EARTH
KEEPING

EARTH KEEPING

MAKING IT A FAMILY HABIT

SYDNEY L. DONAHOE

ZondervanPublishingHouse
Grand Rapids, Michigan

A Division of HarperCollins*Publishers*

Earth Keeping
Making It a Family Habit
Copyright © 1990 by Sydney Donahoe
All rights reserved

Published by Zondervan Publishing House
1415 Lake Drive, S.E., Grand Rapids, Michigan 49506

Library of Congress Cataloging-in-Publication Data

Donahoe, Sydney.
    Earth keeping / by Sydney Donahoe.
      p. cm.
    Includes bibliographical references.
    ISBN 0-310-53801-7
    1. Environmental protection—Citizen participation. 2. Christian life—
1960– I. Title.
    TD171.7.D64   1991
    363.7'0525—dc–20   91–20125
                                               CIP

The information in this book was gathered from a variety of sources, all of which the author and publisher believe to be reliable and accurate. We can't and don't guarantee the results, however. The responsibility for using the ideas in this book, and using them in a safe manner, rests entirely with the reader or user. This book is meant to be both thought-provoking and informative, but no liability on the part of author or publisher is implied.

Cover designed by The Aslan Group, LTD.
Cover illustration by Mark Herron
Interior designed by Rachel Hostetter

Printed in the United States of America

91 92 93 94 95 / ML / 10 9 8 7 6 5 4 3 2 1

 **Printed on Recycled Paper**

To my parents
Earth Keeping *is just another phrase
for what you've always called
"saving" and "not wasting."
I recall your many good examples
with a new appreciation.*

A SPECIAL
THANKS

To Barb Walker for her very good idea.

To Steve Walker for generously sharing his knowledge of the Bible.

To Pegi Harvey for helping me learn to say "I can."

To Jim Donahoe for all those finishing touches and so much more.

To Jessi and Shannon for sharing me with my computer.

And to all these wonderful people whose input is so evident to me as I read the finished manuscript:

Kim Crocker
Sylvia Edwards
Eloy and Becky Garcia
Susan Hand
Cindy Harris
Rosemary Hawver
Alison Hawver

Elaine Lee
Lois Lippold
Anne Maley
Tom and Tambra Murphy
Maureen Rogers
Beth Sandler
Jon and Barbara Sandy

CONTENTS

God saw all that he had made,
and it was very good.
GENESIS 1:31

E A R T H   K E E P I N G

Definitions

Earth: the planet on which we live.
Keeping: a reserving or preserving for future use.
Steward: one who actively directs affairs, a manager.
Habit: an acquired mode of behavior that has become nearly or completely involuntary.

1

E A R T H K E E P I N G

How to Use This Book

Even though you are just one person who may never have done anything extraordinary before, you can change the world.
DIANE MACEACHERN
SAVE OUR PLANET

❏ Many people care about the earth

Who doesn't care about the environment? In recent years you don't have to be a nature lover to be concerned about pollution, global warming, and acid rain. Anyone who reads newspapers or watches television knows our planet is beginning to show disastrous signs of environmental abuse.

❏ Earth keeping goes beyond caring

Today's ecological problems seem so overwhelming. Can just one person help avoid global disaster? Yes. You—together with millions of other individuals with earth-friendly habits—can make a significant difference.

As an individual, how can you contribute positively to the future of planet Earth? Brace yourself; you probably know what's coming. Yes, you'll need to make a few changes.

Now wait—before you panic and decide to recycle this book, let me assure you that I know how hard it is to add even one more task to your busy schedule. My life is like that too. That's why this book's unique format can help you add some new ecological habits to your life at your own pace and as painlessly as possible.

You probably already have some helpful habits. As you read through this book, you're likely to identify things you're already doing. That's great. Congratulate yourself. Check off those habits, and keep at them.

But you'll also discover some new behaviors. Choose 1 or 2 to add to your daily routine. Determine to make them a permanent part of your life. Gradually add a few more new habits. Of course, the faster you add earth-friendly behaviors, the better, but the main goal is to make permanent changes—ones that last.

❏ Your family may notice new behaviors

Chapters 2 to 11 are tailored to help you learn new place-oriented, earth-friendly habits—in your kitchen, your bathroom, your car. . . . Each of these chapters ends with a checklist summary of the suggested earth-keeping habits.

In the last chapter of the book, you'll find a second set of the habit checklists, which you can remove and post—on the refrigerator, on the bathroom mirror, on your car's visor. . . . Having these lists visible will remind you—and your family—to act on your new goals.

Your family will begin noticing your new habits too. In the car, at dinner, or in the midst of a new habit, you'll have opportunities to talk with them about the changes you're making. Before long, they will want to make changes too. Let them check the lists as they become better stewards of the earth. Someone in your family may even emerge as an "environmental watchdog." In our family it's the 7-year-old who spots leaky faucets and misplaced trash.

❏ We need to learn new habits in 4 areas

There are thousands of ways to practice good stewardship of the earth. But books cannot go on forever. I've chosen to list behaviors that will have an effect in at least 1 of 4 areas:

● saving energy—conserving our limited natural gas, oil, and petroleum resources and more effectively combatting pollution, acid rain, and global warming;

● reducing waste—getting at the problem of overflowing landfills, depletion of natural resources, and unnecessary pollution by reducing our use of "throwaways," by reusing and recycling products;

● conserving water—using groundwater (underground water that is not quickly replenished by rain or snow, and supplies more than 90% of our drinking water) less wastefully, polluting oceans, lakes and streams less, and easing up on the excessive demands we place on overburdened sewage systems;

● lessening our direct negative impact on nature—reducing litter, habitat destruction, species extinction, and chemical contamination.

Focusing attention on these 4 areas can have a big payoff in terms of preserving our planet.

❏ It's worth it

Is all this fuss about the environment really necessary? Based on the evidence provided by our planet, most experts think so. After reading some of the statistics in this book, you'll probably agree.

One thing is certain: Changing our behavior to conserve Earth's resources can't hurt. Even small changes might add up to something that refreshes and rejuvenates our planet. And making small changes now could help prepare us for more drastic changes we eventually might be forced to make.

❏ Is ecology in the Bible?

Don't try to find *biodegradable* or *chlorofluorocarbons* in your concordance. But the principles of ecology are definitely in the Bible.

At any point in your reading, you might flip to chapter 12, "Earth Keeping and the Christian Lifestyle," which shows that there is nothing new about an ecology-conscious lifestyle and good stewardship. Jesus himself provided a model for responsible living. Should some of your new habits be questioned by those around you, remember that Jesus never hesitated to buck the status quo to set something right.

❏ Handy glossary is provided for your reference

Chapter 13 provides further explanation of terms in this book, including acid rain, global warming, and ozone smog. If you come across something you don't understand, turn to the alphabetical glossary for clarification.

❏ Keep it simple, steward

Use *Earth Keeping* in the way that works best for you. As you add new behaviors to your life, remember that all of your new earth-keeping habits

● will help the environment;

● are most effective if they're permanent;

● can be passed on to others.

The earth is the Lord's, and everything in it.
PSALM 24:1

2

EART**H KE**EPING

in Your
Kitchen

Gather the pieces that are left over. Let nothing be wasted.
JOHN 6:12

Jesus calls us to a no-waste lifestyle. Does that mean we should stop eating meat? Possibly. Does it mean we should eat less meat? Probably. Does it mean we should not waste food? Positively.
STANLEY C. BALDWIN
CHRISTIANITY TODAY
(JULY 16, 1976)

We generate 160 million tons of rubbish a year. . . . A convoy of 10-ton garbage trucks carrying the nation's annual waste would reach halfway to the moon.
DAN GROSSMAN AND
SETH SHULMAN
DISCOVER (APRIL 1990)

❑ **Rinse dishes in a pan, not under running water**

If you wash dishes by hand—rather than with a dishwasher—you can save water, under certain conditions. On average, dishwashers use almost 10 gallons of water per load. Washing by hand uses 5 to 20 gallons. People who manage to use 5 gallons (or less) turn the water off while they're rinsing.

I start rinsing dishes under running water, which I catch in a dishpan. By the time the dishpan is half-full of water, I've got half the dishes rinsed. Then I turn off the water and rinse the other dishes in the pan.

❑ Use energy-efficient cycles on your dishwasher. Wash full loads. Air dry dishes.

If you run 1 load of dishes a day, a dishwasher will probably use less water than you would washing dishes by hand several times a day. Be sure you wash only full loads of dishes.

If your dishwasher has a water-heating option, deselect it. Then the dishwasher will use water at the temperature delivered by your water heater (set at 130 degrees); it will not expend extra energy heating the water to 140 degrees. The water will still be hot enough to kill germs and get dishes clean. To dry dishes, select "air dry," or at the beginning of the drying mode shut off the dishwasher and open the door, allowing dishes to air dry. Use any other energy-efficient cycles (e.g., "light wash") available on your dishwasher.

❑ Use spatula—not running water—to remove food from dishes

Before you wash dishes or load the dishwasher, scrape food from the dishes into a compost pail or trash can rather than rinse the dishes under running water. You can save as much as 5 gallons this way every time you do dishes. That savings can add up to 15 or more gallons a day. You'll save water and also energy by reducing your need to run the garbage disposal.

❑ Keep a bottle of drinking water in the refrigerator

In the U.S. people use about 450 billion gallons of water every day. Since your kitchen faucet pumps out at least 5 gallons of water a minute, you can easily waste 2 gallons just waiting for the water to get cold for a drink.

Instead, keep a bottle of water in the refrigerator—near the front, so you don't have to leave the door open to hunt around for it. If that doesn't work for you, you might pop a few ice cubes into a glass of water to cool it quickly.

❏ **Set your refrigerator thermostat at 38 to 42 degrees; keep it clean and in good repair; open it as little as possible**

Refrigerators consume about 7% of the total energy used annually in the United States. To get the most for your energy expenditure, set the refrigerator temperature between 38 and 42 degrees and the freezer compartment between 0 and 5 degrees. For every degree below these temperatures, your refrigerator's energy consumption goes up by about 2%.

Keeping your refrigerator clean inside and out also helps efficiency. Clean the condenser coils on the back or bottom with a vacuum or brush. Make sure the door seal is tight, and keep the freezer well defrosted.

Each of the world's 50 million refrigerators contains up to 2.5 lbs. of chlorofluorocarbons (CFCs), trapped in insulation and held in condenser units. These CFCs have the potential, if released, to do unimaginable damage to the earth's protective ozone layer. So if your refrigerator needs repair, be sure to use a service that captures CFCs that may be released during servicing. Sometimes this aspect of service is called "vapor recovery" or "emission control." If you must discard your refrigerator, make sure its ultimate destination is a recycling center that will capture and recycle the CFCs contained in it.

The less you open your refrigerator, the colder it stays. So when you're baking, cooking dinner, or making lunches, try to take out all the ingredients at one time, then put them all away at the same time.

❏ Use the stove, microwave, toaster oven, or pressure cooker instead of a conventional oven

Use the smallest possible appliance for cooking. For example, simmering a pan on an 8-inch stove-burner for an hour uses one-eighth the energy of an oven set at 350 degrees for 1 hour. A microwave oven, which uses about the same amount of energy as a conventional oven, cooks most foods in less than half the time—so you save half the energy. A pressure cooker can cut cooking time and energy use by about two-thirds.

❏ Bake several items at once; keep your oven closed

Since your oven is a big energy consumer, try to get the most out of it every time you use it. If you have freezer space, bake multiple batches of cookies and casseroles. Bake extra potatoes to use the next day for hash browns. If you're cooking a roast, why not make muffins too? While things are baking, resist the urge to peek inside. Every time you do, you lose 25 degrees of heat. Instead, look through the glass window if your oven has one, or use a timer.

❏ Eat—and serve—less meat

If you are a confirmed meat eater, brace yourself for some surprising facts:

- Half the forests in Central America and 25 million acres of forests in Brazil have been cleared away for cattle ranches

- It takes 2,500 gallons of water to produce a pound of beef, but 25 gallons of water to produce a pound of wheat.

- More than 40% of the world's grain goes to feed livestock, not people.

- An acre of land can produce up to 667 pounds of protein if planted in soybeans. If planted for livestock feed, it ultimately yields 97 pounds of protein in chicken, 29 pounds of protein in pork, and a mere 9 pounds of protein in beef.

- If Americans were to eat just 10% less meat per year, the grain saved could feed 60 million people—the number of people who now starve to death each year.

World hunger will not be solved simply by your eating less meat. Politics and food distribution systems complicate solutions to the problem. But by reducing demand for beef and other meats, Americans can take a step toward becoming less greedy and more willing to do their share in rectifying some wrongs on our planet. Discover the wealth of tasty, healthful eating available in reduced-meat cooking.

❏ Use cloth—not paper—napkins, towels, and rags

Stop for a minute and consider the fact that all paper products come from trees. Then multiply your paper use by all the other homes like yours. That adds up to 42.5 million tons of disposable paper and paperboard products that Americans send to landfills annually, usually after just one use. It seems almost miraculous that we have any trees left.

In your kitchen there are many ways to save paper. Hang a rag on a cup hook or towel rack inside the door under your sink. Wipe up spills on the floor with the rag instead of a paper towel. Rinse the rag between cleanups; periodically wash it.

Use cloth dishtowels, not paper disposables. Use cloth napkins whenever possible. Each member of your family can probably use the same one for several meals, since they're larger and more absorbent. Place the napkin on its user's chair or in a color-keyed napkin ring, ready for the next meal. If you use paper napkins, tear napkins in half for snacks or small meals. Pack lunches in reusable containers, not paper bags.

Using less paper is one good way to reduce the 4 to 6 pounds of trash produced per person per day in the United States.

❏ Store food in reusable containers

Rather than reach for a plastic bag or piece of plastic wrap, reach for a reusable glass, ceramic, or plastic container. When you purchase food in plastic or glass containers (e.g., margarine, cottage cheese, peanut butter), wash and reuse the containers. Pack lunch items in reusable containers with lids that seal tightly, rather than in throwaway sandwich bags. This can help us make better use of the 200 pounds of plastic used by the average U.S. consumer each year.

❏ Use cold water instead of hot whenever possible

One-fifth of the energy used in your home goes to heat water. In the past, I often unnecessarily turned on the hot water tap. Now, I use cold water instead of hot for:

• rinsing my hands, unless they're greasy;

• rinsing out the dishcloth to clean the stove or table;

• rinsing dishes.

No doubt you can find many other ways to use cold water instead of hot. Whenever you avoid using hot water, you save energy.

❏ Fit pots to burners and amounts of food; use lids

When you use a pot or pan that's smaller than the burner or larger than necessary for the portion of food you're heating, you let heat escape; you waste energy. To use your stove most efficiently, choose a clean, unwarped pan that fits or is larger than the burner. Put a lid on the pan; bring liquids to a boil quickly; then turn down the temperature.

❏ Use a permanent coffee filter, not disposables

If you use bleached-paper coffee filters, you risk contaminating your coffee and your body with dioxins, chemicals—some of which are extremely harmful—used in the paper-bleaching process. When hot water seeps through the filter, some residual dioxins seep into your coffee.

Buying permanent, reusable metal or cloth coffee filters helps you and the environment in 3 ways: You avoid spreading dioxins; you avoid consuming dioxins; you reduce your consumption of paper products. See page 126 for addresses of companies that provide mail-order, environment-friendly kitchen supplies.

❏ Line trash cans with newspapers or paper bags instead of plastic

Unfortunately, there is no easy solution to discarding household trash. Problems are evident with every alternative: Plastic is not biodegradable. Biodegradable plastic bags made with cellulose may disintegrate, but cellulose-eating bacteria leave behind plastic "dust" that will never decompose. Paper decomposes slowly in landfills. Photodegradable bags do not decompose in dark, sunless landfills.

In light of all these poor choices, and until we have a better solution, the most acceptable trashcan liner is a newspaper or paper bag. At least paper is biodegradable and comes from trees, a renewable resource; any plastic choice is nonbiodegradable and uses oil, a nonrenewable resource.

The best choice, of course, is to use no liners in trash cans. This option is most workable if you compost kitchen waste. If your refuse-disposal service allows the use of garbage cans without bags, simply rinse out the cans after they're dumped.

❑ Cut the rings on plastic holders of 6-pack cans

Those plastic holders for 6-packs of canned drinks often find their way into rivers, lakes, and oceans. They're washed off beaches, dumped into water with garbage, or carried by birds or the wind. In the water, animals become entangled in the plastic rings and die slow and excruciating deaths from starvation, drowning, or strangulation. Plastic rings constitute a small part of an estimated 14 billion pounds of trash dumped into the sea every year.

Before discarding the plastic packaging of beverages purchased in 6-packs, snip open any circles formed by the plastic. Better yet, buy drinks that aren't joined by plastic rings. If you find plastic rings on the beach or in a park, pick them up and dispose of them correctly.

❏ Recycle aluminum, glass, cardboard, and plastic

Of all the earth-friendly, good-steward activities you can do, recycling has the biggest environmental payoff. It conserves resources and reduces energy use; recycling can cut a household's stream of waste by 80%. At our house, recycling just these 4 materials reduced our trash output by half:

Aluminum: Aluminum is made from bauxite ore, mined mostly in tropical forests in countries such as Guinea, Australia, and Brazil. One of the most expensive and polluting materials ever made, aluminum is also one of the most recyclable. Making a recycled aluminum can uses 95% less energy than making a can from raw materials. Every time you recycle an aluminum can, you're saving enough energy to run a TV for 3 hours. Americans currently recycle more than half of their aluminum drink cans. And aluminum recycling is fast: The can you buy today was probably recycled by someone just 6 to 12 weeks ago.

Today 95% of all beverage cans are aluminum and can be recycled in drop-off centers, buy-back locations, or reverse vending machines. But a few cans are still made of steel. If you're unsure about a can, hold a magnet to its side; magnets won't stick to aluminum. If you have steel cans, you can recycle them separately from aluminum cans, but recycling centers don't pay you for them.

Don't forget about the other aluminum you use, most of which is recyclable. See if you can find a recycling center near you that accepts aluminum pie pans, foil, frozen-food trays, window frames, and siding. Remember, with every can and piece of foil you recycle, you are making a big difference.

Glass: Glass, like aluminum, is 100% recyclable. If you recycle glass containers, you can reduce your household waste by about 10%. In addition, glass made from recycled instead of raw material reduces related air pollution by 20% and water pollution by 50%.

Check with your local recycling centers to learn how to sort your glass items. Most centers require separation of colored and clear glass, and some require removal of aluminum neck rings or lids. Your center may accept other kinds of glass too, such as plate glass. If not, remember: Even if you recycle glass jars only, each one will save enough energy to light a 100-watt light bulb for 4 hours.

Cardboard and paper: Cardboard and paper, like aluminum and glass, are fully recyclable. In 1989 Americans recycled over 27 million tons of paper and cardboard products. But we used more than 3 times that amount: a total of 86 million tons.

You can improve our recycling record by taking cardboard cartons, used envelopes, and used writing paper to a recycling center. Some centers want colored paper sorted from white paper or plastic windows removed from envelopes. Check with your center to find out their specifications.

Plastic: Plastic recycling presents some problems not posed by paper, aluminum, or glass. Not all types of plastic are recyclable, and recycled plastic can usually be reused a limited number of times. With plastic, it's best to "precycle"— choose not to purchase items made from or packaged in plastic. When you do have plastic containers, however, these 4 types of plastic are most commonly recycled:

Polyethylene terephthalate (PET or PETE—marked as ♲) is used in about 25% of all plastic bottles, including clear plastic bottles that hold dish detergent and cleaning products. Plastic soda bottles are made from it, as are bags for boil-in-bag foods. About 20% of the 750 million pounds of

PET plastic bottles used each year is recycled—into carpet fibers, nonfood bottles, fiberfill, and polyester.

High-density polyethylene (HDPE—marked as ♲) is used in opaque or colored plastic bottles that hold milk, detergents, shampoos, bottled water, bleach, paper wipes, and antifreeze, and in some types of plastic bags. HDPE plastic can be recycled into products like plastic lumber, trash cans, flowerpots, toys, and base cups for plastic soda-bottles.

Polyvinyl chloride (PVC—marked as ♲) is used in bottles that hold edible oils, liquor, and some types of shampoo and food. It's best to avoid this type of packaging, as very little of it is being recycled. When it is recycled, it can be used in products like pipes, vinyl floor tiles, and truck-bed liners.

Low-density polyethylene (LDPE—marked as ♲) is used to make the plastic bags used for bread, produce, and laundry. Recycling programs for this type of plastic are just beginning. You're likely to notice drop-off bins for plastic bags in grocery stores. Check with your local recycling centers to find out what types of plastic you can recycle. When you begin recycling, you'll want to designate containers so you can sort various recyclable items. You can use simple cardboard boxes, or you can purchase specially designed recycling bins. Mark the containers so your family will know what to put where. Before long, everyone at your house will automatically recycle much of the trash you used to throw away. For general help in getting started with recycling, see the resources on page 126.

Earth Keeping in Your Kitchen

- ☐ Rinse dishes in a pan, not under running water.
- ☐ Use energy-efficient cycles on your dishwasher. Wash full loads. Air dry dishes.
- ☐ Use a spatula—not running water—to remove food from dishes.
- ☐ Keep a bottle of drinking water in the refrigerator.
- ☐ Set your refrigerator thermostat at 38 to 42 degrees. Keep it clean and in good repair. Open it as little as possible.
- ☐ Use the stove, microwave, toaster oven, or pressure cooker instead of a conventional oven.
- ☐ Bake several items at once; keep your oven closed.
- ☐ Eat—and serve—less meat.
- ☐ Use cloth—not paper—napkins, towels, and rags.
- ☐ Store food in reusable containers.
- ☐ Use cold water instead of hot whenever possible.
- ☐ Fit pots to burners and amounts of food; use lids.
- ☐ Use a permanent coffee filter, not disposables.
- ☐ Line trash cans with newspapers or paper bags instead of plastic.
- ☐ Cut the rings on plastic holders of 6-pack cans.
- ☐ Recycle aluminum, glass, cardboard, and plastic.

You'll find a removable copy of this checklist on page 125.

3

E A R T H K E E P I N G

in Your

Living Room

You are worthy, our Lord and God,
*   to receive glory and honor and power,*
for you created all things,
*   and by your will they were created*
*   and have their being.*

REVELATION 4:11

Where Christian tradition has contributed toward abuses, repen-
tance is needed and a new example required as a matter of
urgency.

RON ELSDON, *BENT WORLD*

For the majority of Americans . . . making peace with the environ-
ment means undergoing a gradual learning and change process
that will lead us to a comfortable and non-destructive way of life.

THE BENNETT INFORMATION
GROUP, *THE GREEN PAGES*

❏ Recycle your newspapers

The United States runs ahead of the rest of the world in paper
use but trails far behind in paper recycling. We use more
than 67 tons of paper each year. That's almost 600 pounds
per person. Yet we recycle only about one-third of that.

Recycling newspapers is easy and has a big impact on the
environment. If you recycle your daily newspaper for a year,
you'll save the equivalent of 4 trees, keep 15 pounds of
pollutants out of the atmosphere, conserve 2,200 gallons of
water, and save enough energy to light a 100-watt light bulb
for 5 months. Also, making recycled paper uses less bleach

and fewer chemicals than making new paper. In addition to conserving natural resources, reducing energy, and cutting waste and chemicals, producing a ton of recycled paper can create 5 times more jobs than producing a ton of paper from virgin wood pulp.

Check your area for newspaper drop-off locations. Some recyclers require that you separate "slick" supplement sections from the regular newsprint. Find out if your recycler prefers you to box, stack, tie, or bag the papers. If you have difficulty finding a place to recycle newsprint, it's probably because fewer than 10 newsprint mills in North America are trying to handle the entire country's newspaper recycling load. Because of growing consumer demand, however, more mills are being constructed. If you have difficulty recycling newspaper now, be patient. It should become easier in the near future.

❏ Share magazine and newspaper subscriptions

If you save 4 trees a year by recycling your newspapers, why not save 8 trees by sharing your paper with a neighbor? And why not share magazine subscriptions? Find a friend who subscribes to a magazine you enjoy. Offer to share the cost in exchange for a chance to read. Or trade off issues of a magazine you receive. Do you know a doctor, dentist, or counselor who could use your magazines in a waiting room? Libraries often accept magazines for check-out or sale. When magazines have outlived their use, recycle them with "mixed paper" in your curbside bin or try to find a drop-off recycling center that accepts them.

❏ Close the fireplace damper when you're not using your fireplace

If your heater or furnace runs while your fireplace damper is open, up to 8% of your heat can go right up your chimney.

Close the damper to keep warm furnace-air from escaping (or, if your fireplace has glass doors or a woodstove, keep the doors closed). But be sure to open the damper before you build your next fireplace fire.

❏ Use your fireplace rarely; consider installing a wood-burning stove or fireplace insert

All fireplaces put carbon dioxide into the air and contribute to air pollution. In addition, most fireplaces suck more warm air out through the chimney than they put into the room.

If you plan to use a fireplace often, seriously consider purchasing a woodstove or energy-efficient fireplace insert. Purchase a model that has a secondary burn chamber or catalytic device that reduces harmful emissions, so your fires pollute less. In addition, a woodstove can be up to 65% efficient in delivering energy in the form of heat, while fireplaces are usually only 10% efficient.

When selecting wood to burn, choose dense species, such as oak, birch, and ash, which have a high heating value. Softer woods, like pine and fir, do not give off as much heat when they burn; that means you get less heat for the energy used and the pollution produced.

❏ Turn heat or air conditioning to the temperature you want, not higher or lower

For the average home 50% to 70% of the energy consumed goes to home heating and cooling. It only makes sense to use your heater and air conditioner efficiently. When you walk into a cold room in the winter, resist the urge to turn the thermostat higher than your ultimate desired temperature. The higher setting won't heat the room faster, but once the room is above your desired temperature, you're wasting energy. And it's easy to forget you turned it higher, running the furnace for an extended period of time.

The same is true for cooling a room. A cooler-than-desired thermostat setting won't cool the room faster. It may be a challenge to get this "lesson" through to the more impatient members of your family, particularly teenagers.

❏ Clean and replace your air conditioner and furnace filters regularly

When actively running your air conditioner or furnace, it's best to clean or change the filters every month. An air conditioner or furnace fan has to run longer to move the same amount of air through a dirty filter than through a clean one. See page 128 for resources that give more information on efficient home use of energy.

❏ Keep home air-conditioning equipment in good repair. Make sure vapors are recovered during servicing

Home air conditioners (both window and central) contain hydrochlorofluorocarbons (HCFCs). Heat pumps (another method of cooling your home) also contain HCFCs. HCFCs are "second generation" chlorofluorocarbons (CFCs). Although HCFCs are 95% less damaging to the ozone than CFCs, they still pose a threat. Make sure your home air-conditioning equipment is in good repair. If it needs servicing, make sure the technician does not release HCFCs into the air, but rather captures them with vapor recovery equipment.

❏ At night and when you leave home for several hours: In winter lower your furnace thermostat setting; in summer raise your air-conditioner setting

The energy it takes to light, heat, and cool just 1 home for 1 year can put more than 10 tons of carbon dioxide into the atmosphere—contributing to global warming. The fastest way to reduce this impact on the environment is to use less heat and air conditioning. If you're going out for a few hours, turn your furnace down or your air conditioner up 6 to 10 degrees. You can readjust the thermostat when you return home, but you saved energy while you were gone.

If you don't want to rely on your memory, you might also consider installing a programmable thermostat for your furnace or air conditioner. You can set this device to adjust the temperature automatically at night or at times when you're regularly out of the house (e.g., during the day, if you go to work).

If you can stay warm enough by heating only the room you're using (rather than the entire house or apartment), you can save energy by using a space heater, if it's an energy-efficient model. Good choices in space heaters include window-box solar room heaters and natural-gas-fueled space heaters that are externally vented.

Unfortunately, the easiest-to-use space heaters are not usually the most efficient. By and large, electric space heaters are poor choices because they guzzle energy—and usually at peak times. If you must use an electric space heater, radiant types are probably the best energy choice, since they warm people and objects rather than the air in a room. Before you invest in a space heater of any kind, however, consider saftey factors, especially if children are in your home. Look for models with safety features like tipover switches (which automatically shut off the heater if it tips over) and on/off signal lights.

❑ **In winter open drapes to let in sunshine; in summer close them against the sunshine**

In winter you can warm up a room by opening shades and drapes to let the sun in. Be sure to close them at night, though, to help retain the heat. The reverse is true in the summer: Close your drapes against the sun, then open them at night to let cool air in. You might consider purchasing insulated drapes. In the winter hanging a blanket over a window can help insulate it.

❑ **Install ceiling fans to circulate air**

If you use an air conditioner, you might be able to use it less often or get by with a higher temperature setting if you install a ceiling fan. For about as much energy as a 100-watt light bulb, a ceiling fan allows you to maintain a comfort level while raising your air conditioner's thermostat as much as 5 degrees—saving considerable energy.

A ceiling fan can save energy in the winter too, if it has a reverse switch that enables the fan to push warm air down from the ceiling to lower areas of the room.

❑ **Dress warmer in winter and cooler in summer to minimize the use of heaters and air conditioners**

In winter set your thermostat between 68 and 70 degrees, then dress in warm clothing. For every degree you set your thermostat below 68.6, you save 3% on your heating costs. At

68 degrees, most people need a sweater to be comfortable. Dressing in layers helps too.

In the summer try to keep your thermostat no lower than 78 degrees, and dress in cool clothing. If you set your thermostat even higher than 78, you'll save 5% in energy costs for each degree. Even if you keep your thermostat at 78—as opposed to 72—you could lower your cooling costs by as much as 40%.

❑ Use compact fluorescent light bulbs wherever you can; install dimmer switches on other fixtures

Compact fluorescent light bulbs come in several shapes to fit a variety of sockets and provide light similar to incandescent light. If you've ever priced compact fluorescent light bulbs, you know they're more expensive than incandescent (plain old) bulbs. But a single compact fluorescent bulb is actually more economical, as it can last 10 times longer than a regular bulb and uses one-fourth the energy. Being so energy efficient, it prevents over its lifetime the power-plant emission of half a ton of carbon dioxide into the atmosphere.

If compact fluorescents don't fit into all your fixtures, consider installing dimmer switches on fixtures that use incandescent lights. You'll be saving energy and extending the life of your bulbs. See page 132 for resources that can help you light your home efficiently.

❑ Avoid buying furniture and accessories made from tropical woods

Tropical forests once carpeted about 5 billion acres of our planet. Less than half those forests still stand. A whopping 80% of the destruction has occurred since 1980. Almost

80,000 acres a day fall to loggers or are cleared for farms or cattle ranches. Even though this destruction happens primarily in underdeveloped countries (where tropical forests are located), it is caused by people like us who demand products made from tropical woods—teak, mahogany, rosewood, ebony, iroko, and lauan—imported from tropical forest areas.

Why does it matter that tropical forests are disappearing? Here are just a few of many reasons:

Species diversity: Scientists estimate that tropical forests are home to half the living species. Aside from their basic right to share our planet, many of these species are sources of food and life-saving medicines. For example, a drug we derive from Madagascar's rosy periwinkle plant gives lymphocytic leukemia victims a 99% chance of recovery. So far, scientists have analyzed only 1% of identified tropical forest plants, but even this small percentage is the source of one-fourth to one-half of all medical compounds sold today.

Carbon dioxide consumption: One deciduous tree can consume from 16 to 48 pounds of carbon dioxide every year. You can see why losing 100 acres of tropical forest a minute—almost a football field every second—has a devastating effect on our atmosphere. Carbon dioxide is responsible for 50% of global warming. To make matters worse, many of those tropical forest acres are burned, not logged; we not only lose the trees that consume carbon dioxide, but the burning itself adds tons of carbon dioxide to the atmosphere.

Source of food crops: Approximately half the world's leading food crops have their origins in tropical forest plants. About 12 of these crops provide 90% of the food consumed by humans around the world, including rice and maize. We may need to return to tropical forests for additional food crop species as our world's population continues to grow. And disease- and pest-resistant tropical forest plants may boost our domestic crops' rate of production.

The next time you're ready to purchase furniture or accessories for your home, buy ash, beech, birch, cherry, elm, hickory, oak, poplar, or black walnut; avoid all tropical woods. (See page 128 for a list of tropical woods.) If you don't know what kind of wood a product is made of, ask. And be on the lookout for tropical wood in unlikely places. For instance, chopsticks provided by take-out restaurants or sold by the gross are often made from Indonesian hardwoods.

Earth Keeping in Your Living Room

❑ Recycle your newspapers.

❑ Share magazine and newspaper subscriptions.

❑ Close the fireplace damper when you're not using your fireplace.

❑ Use your fireplace rarely; consider installing a wood-burning stove or fireplace insert.

❑ Turn heat or air conditioning to the temperature you want, not higher or lower.

❑ Clean and replace air conditioner and furnace filters regularly.

❑ Keep home air-conditioning equipment in good repair. Make sure vapors are recovered during servicing.

❑ At night and when you leave home for several hours: In winter lower your furnace thermostat setting. In summer raise your air conditioner setting.

❑ In winter open drapes to let in sunshine. In summer close them against the sunshine.

❑ Install ceiling fans to circulate air.

❑ Dress warmer in winter and cooler in summer to minimize the use of heaters and air conditioners.

❑ Use compact fluorescent light bulbs wherever you can; install dimmer switches on other fixtures.

❑ Avoid buying furniture and accessories made from tropical hardwoods.

You'll find a removable copy of this checklist on page 127.

EARTHKEEPING

in Your

Bathroom

You care for the land and water it;
  you enrich it abundantly.
The streams of God are filled with water
  to provide the people with grain,
  for so you have ordained it.

PSALM 65:9

. . . sustainability requires that we relate to the realm of nature in ways that respect its integrity, so that natural systems may continue to function properly, the earth's beauty and fruitfulness may be maintained and kept sufficient for human sustenance, and life may continue also for the nonhuman species.

PRESBYTERIAN ECO-JUSTICE
TASK FORCE, *KEEPING AND
HEALING THE CREATION*

Every day, Americans flush more than 5 billion gallons of water down the toilet. That's about 3.5 billion gallons more than is actually needed for effective flushing. Americans also shower with 3 billion gallons of water a day, 1.5 billion gallons more than is needed.

CONSUMER REPORTS (JULY 1990)

❏ Take a short shower or a shallow bath

Try to shower in less than 5 minutes or bathe in shallow water. Even a quick shower or a shallow bath can use quite a few gallons of water, so check this chapter for other ways to save while you get clean.

35

❏ Install a low-flow shower head

There's another benefit for conservative water users: a reduction in your utility bills. A low-flow shower head can save an average family 20 to 50 dollars a year by reducing the amount of energy required to heat water. Then there's the 5 to 10 thousand gallons of water saved per year.

Shop carefully and you can find a shower head that will give you a good shower yet flow at only 3 gallons per minute. Check the *Consumer Reports*, July 1990, to help you choose a model.

❏ Use less shampoo, conditioner, deodorant, and soap

Today's environmental by-words are *reduce, reuse, recycle.* In the bathroom, there are plenty of opportunities to reduce use. Try cutting by half the shampoo you pour into your palm, and lather up once, not twice. See how little conditioner, deodorant, and soap you can use and still get the job done. You'll be saving the resources needed to make that product and the energy used in manufacturing it. And you'll be reducing the chemical and soapy residue that gets washed down your drain.

❏ Turn off the water while you lather your hair and body in the shower, brush your teeth, and shave

Studies show that the average American uses more than 60 gallons of water every day, three-fourths of it in the bathroom. Can you imagine life in some countries where people regularly live on 4 or fewer gallons a day? And what of the thousands of people who die daily from lack of water to raise crops, feed livestock, or drink? Isn't it reasonable that we should turn off the water while we enjoy the luxuries of soaping up in the shower or brushing away at our teeth? A simple flick of the wrist can save 10 gallons per brushing (even more, if you use water in a glass) and 7 gallons per minute in the shower.

Teach your children good-steward hygiene habits when they're young—before they lock you out of the bathroom.

❏ Turn on the water less than full force when rinsing your hands, teeth, or body

Most faucets, turned on full force, pump out at least 5 gallons of water per minute. You can easily save water by simply turning the faucet on less than full force whenever possible. You'll hardly notice the difference when you use less water to rinse your hands or body. (If you do, guard against running the water longer, which of course would defeat the purpose.)

❏ Install faucet aerators

Saving water has 2 favorable outcomes I haven't yet mentioned: As fewer dams are constructed, less damage is wreaked on the environment. In addition, our municipal water systems get a much-needed reprieve from our excessive demands.

Installing a low-flow faucet aerator can save 50% of the water that runs from your sink faucets. Aerators can be deceiving. They mix the air with water and make it seem as if more— not less—water is gushing out. You can find inexpensive, easy-to-install aerators at a hardware store.

❏ **Use products that are packaged most sensibly, for example, toothpaste in a tube, not a pump; sanitary supplies without individual wrapping**

Look at a product and its packaging from an earth-conscious point of view. Is it overpackaged? Is the packaging made from recycled or recyclable material? From toothpaste to toilet paper, make the least wasteful choices in packaging, and be sure to recycle packaging whenever you can.

❏ **Use unscented deodorants, shampoos, lotions, and soaps**

It makes sense: Fewer chemicals go into the manufacture of unscented toiletries. Fewer chemicals touch you. Fewer chemicals rinse off your body and clothes into our water systems. If you prefer scented toiletries, check labels to find products made of natural rather than chemical fragrances. Whenever possible choose biodegradable personal products.

❏ **Avoid using aerosol sprays**

Chlorofluorocarbons (CFCs) are causing grave damage to the ozone layer of the atmosphere. As the ozone deteriorates, harmful rays from the sun can pass through to the earth, causing environmental and health catastrophes. Even though the Environmental Protection Agency banned nonessential use of CFCs in 1978, some aerosols with CFCs are still on the market. It's safest to avoid buying any aerosol spray, since some substitutes for CFCs contribute to smog.

Replacements for aerosol products include natural or roll-on deodorants, herbal potpourri air fresheners, and products in refillable pumps rather than aerosol containers.

❏ Use a permanent razor instead of disposables

Two billion disposable razors and blades are discarded by Americans every year. High quantities of energy and toxic chemicals go into the manufacture of these razors. Because they're plastic, they aren't biodegradable; they just take up space in landfills. Choose a high-quality metal razor and long-lasting blades, or use an electric shaver instead of resource-wasting disposables.

❏ Flush the toilet less often

Your toilet is the biggest water consumer in your home. An average family of 4 flushes the toilet about 20 times a day, using 5 to 7 gallons each time. That's some 140 gallons of water.

What if you made an agreement in your family not to flush the home toilet after every use? You would, of course, want to set a few ground rules to avoid some potentially unpleasant experiences. But if you can come up with a system that's acceptable, your family will be working as a team to save one of earth's most endangered resources.

❏ Keep a bucket in the shower to catch the water you run while you're waiting for it to warm up.

You might feel a little silly standing in the shower, holding a bucket to catch water. But just remind yourself that you're treating one of our most precious resources with the respect it deserves. After your shower, you can use the water you collected to give your indoor or outdoor plants a water-saving shower of their own.

❏ Displace the water in your toilet tank with a jar, bag, or toilet dam

In the U.S. we flush more than 5 billion gallons of water down the toilet every day. That makes any and all toilet water-saving strategies worthwhile. This one can save you up to 2 gallons per flush:

Fill a plastic or glass jar with water. If the container has a metal lid, then find another stopper or lid for it (metal lids could corrode and cause damage or leaks in your toilet). Then place the jar in your toilet tank. You'll have to do some experimenting to make sure the container doesn't interfere with the working parts in the tank. (If your tank is large enough, you can put more than 1 container in it.) You might also check with a hardware store or your local water utility for a water-filled displacement bag that hangs inside the tank. Hardware stores also carry toilet dams—devices you can place in your tank to conserve 1 gallon of water per flush for each dam installed. Choose a method that's easy and work-able for you, and start saving as much as 20 gallons of water a day.

A word of warning: Do not put a brick in your toilet tank. It can disintegrate and clog the working parts of your toilet.

❏ Clean with natural products

Think for a minute about the total amount of household cleaners you might use in a month. It doesn't really seem like much, does it? But it's estimated that the drains of a city of a million people wash down 31 tons of toilet bowl cleaner and 130.75 tons of liquid cleaners each month. Many of these products contain toxic chemicals that have to be dealt with in municipal sewage treatment plants—or they simply find their way into local groundwater, a main source of our drinking water.

There's one simple way to stop this contamination: Stop using toxic products. For instance, you can replace toilet cleaners that release chemicals with every flush with vinegar, baking soda, or borax and a toilet brush.

Read labels and look for warnings. Here's what they mean on household cleaners: POISON = highly toxic; DANGER = extremely flammable, corrosive, or highly toxic; WARNING or CAUTION = less toxic. See page 130 for a more complete list of bathroom cleaning alternatives that can save you money and the earth from further contamination.

Earth Keeping in Your Bathroom

- ☐ Take a short shower or a shallow bath.
- ☐ Install a low-flow shower head.
- ☐ Use less shampoo, conditioner, deodorant, and soap.
- ☐ Turn off the water while you lather your hair and body in the shower, brush your teeth, and shave.
- ☐ Turn on the water less than full force when rinsing your hands, teeth, or body.
- ☐ Install faucet aerators.
- ☐ Use products that are packaged most sensibly, for example, toothpaste in a tube, not a pump; sanitary supplies without individual wrapping.
- ☐ Use unscented deodorants, shampoos, lotions, and soaps.
- ☐ Avoid using aerosol sprays.
- ☐ Use a permanent razor instead of disposables.
- ☐ Flush the toilet less often.
- ☐ Keep a bucket in the shower to catch the water you run while you're waiting for it to warm up.
- ☐ Displace the water in your toilet tank with a jar, bag, or toilet dam.
- ☐ Clean with natural products.

You'll find a removable copy of this checklist on page 129.

5

E A R T H K E E P I N G

in Your

Bedroom and Baby's Room

But you, O God, are my king from of old;
you bring salvation upon the earth. . . .
The day is yours, and yours also the night;
you established the sun and moon.
It was you who set all the boundaries of the earth;
you made both summer and winter.

PSALM 74:12, 16–17

There is hope for us but no easy healing. There is truth but never without search. There is beauty but only in the exercise of discipline and the control of waste. Our lives can be redeemed but only with lasting commitment to live under God's judgment and grace.

DORIS JANZEN LONGACRE
LIVING MORE WITH LESS

The 1990s are bringing, I think, a new sense of awareness that institutions alone can never solve the problems that cumulate from the seemingly inconsequential actions of millions of individuals. But remember: as much as we are the root of the problem, we are also the genesis of its solution.

CHRIS CALWELL, INTRODUCTION
TO *50 SIMPLE THINGS YOU CAN
DO TO SAVE THE EARTH*

❏ Use cedar chips rather than mothballs

Mothballs may seem harmless. But they're made of 100% paradichlorobenzene—a chemical that can cause serious damage to you and your family. It can irritate the nose, throat, and lungs, and prolonged exposure causes serious damage to the liver and kidneys. If a small child were to eat a mothball (they do look like candy), seizures could result.

Instead of mothballs, use cedar chips, cedar sachets, cedar blocks, or other wood chips soaked in real cedar oil. Or you might try other natural moth repellents, such as whole peppercorns or sachets of lavender, rosemary, and mint.

❑ Avoid heating and cooling spare bedrooms

In the winter and summer you can close off unused rooms in your home and save on energy use for heating and cooling. If you have central heating and/or air-conditioning, be sure to close vents in those unused areas.

❑ Sell or give away unwanted clothing

Consider various options for recycling adults' and children's clothing: Trade clothing (especially children's clothes) with friends; buy and sell clothes at garage sales; donate to and shop at AmVets, Goodwill, and the Salvation Army; donate clothes to your church's homeless ministry, or another charitable or relief organization.

If you have something you're sure no one would wear, you might cut it up for cleaning rags. If this still leaves you with more material scraps than you know what to do with, contact your local Salvation Army. They often accept material pieces in any size or quantity.

This is another opportunity to put good stewardship to work in precycling. Before you buy any clothing, determine that it's good quality, that its style will survive the next fickle fashion trend. Ask yourself: Do I really need this?

❏ Reuse unwearable panty hose

Do you know a woman who doesn't have a dozen or so panty hose in various states of wearability? Believe it or not, there are uses for panty hose, even after they've been worn under slacks to hide the runs or uncomfortably worn 2 pairs as one. (Cut off one leg of each pair; wear a double-layer panty.)

Want a few ideas? With a rubber band fasten a "foot" over the end of your washer-draining hose—to catch lint and prevent a clogged drain; strain old paint through panty hose—to catch the lumps; cut strips of panty hose (stretchy and soft) for plant ties; make panty hose "ropes" to tie up newspapers for recycling; stuff pillows and cloth animals with hose; use small pieces of panty hose instead of cotton balls to remove fingernail polish.

Recently 95%-cotton hose and tights have become available. If you can find them, give them a try. Besides being made from natural and renewable fibers, they are more durable than nylon hosiery.

❏ Give excess clothes hangers to a friend or a dry cleaner who will use them

This habit is just a simple way of reusing one more product made from nonrenewable resources. A local thrift store might appreciate donations.

❏ Choose natural fibers for sheets, towels, and clothing

Nylon, polyester, acrylic. They're words often seen on labels of clothing and linens. What do they mean? These fibers are made from soft, petroleum-based plastics. Using renewable resources is preferable to using up nonrenewable resources, such as oil. Besides that, in some people these fabrics cause toxic symptoms, such as skin rash and eye irritation. For clothing, choose fabrics made from renewable resources, such as cotton, linen, rayon, and wool.

Popular terms like *permanent-press, no-iron,* and *wrinkle-resistant* signal that the material has been treated with a formaldehyde resin. The material may not wrinkle, but as long as the fabric holds together the formaldehyde continues to release fumes. If you or someone in your family suffers headaches, insomnia, tiredness, coughing, watery eyes, or aggravated asthma attacks, consider choosing "Green Cotton" (100% cotton—unbleached, undyed, and without formaldehyde) for your pillowcases, sheets, and towels.

❏ Refuse to purchase clothing or accessories made from wild animals

When you purchase products made from wildlife, you may be contributing to species extinction. For example, the world's demand for ivory could cause the extinction of elephants within the next 20 years unless quick and effective measures are taken to protect these unique animals. During the 1980s, over half of Africa's 1.5 million elephants were slaughtered for ivory. There are fewer than 700,000 left, and they're being killed at the rate of 200 or 300 a day. This tragic loss is because consumers, especially tourists, buy ivory jewelry and trinkets and because importers demand ivory for statues, piano keys, billiard balls, and beads. Today the elephant's future is really in the hands of people—poachers, ivory exporters and importers, and ivory artisans and their customers.

Here are some other wildlife items to avoid as you purchase: anything made from tortoiseshell, wildlife skins (including reptile), furs, coral, sea rocks, and shells. When you see these things for sale, express disapproval to the manufacturer or store manager. The only way to save some of the most cherished animals on earth—including elephants, wildcats, and all kinds of sea creatures—is by putting an end to our demand for products that cost their lives.

❏ Use 1 large bulb rather than 2 smaller bulbs in a multibulb light fixture

A 100-watt bulb can brighten your bedroom as much as 2 60-watt bulbs. But there's one big difference: The single 100-watt bulb uses up to 15% less energy. Check your light fixtures to make sure they can handle the wattage, then try this single-bulb energy-reducing strategy. Better yet, save even more energy and install a lower-wattage compact fluorescent bulb in place of the 100-watt incandescent bulb.

Safety note: If small children or pets can reach the fixture, consider leaving a burned-out bulb in the empty socket.

❏ Turn off the light when you leave the room

When you turn off a light, you cast a vote against global warming and acid rain. That's because when we reduce our demand for energy from coal-, oil-, and natural-gas-burning power plants, we reduce the amount of harmful gases they emit—gases that cause global warming and acid rain.

Is it better to turn off a light if you're going to be out of the room for just a short time? *World Watch* magazine lists these recommendations by Rising Sun Enterprises (a lighting consultant group): Switch off an incandescent bulb if you're going to be out of a room more than 5 minutes; a standard fluorescent, 15 minutes; and a compact fluorescent, more than 30 minutes. If you're in doubt, turn it out.

When you're teaching young children to turn out lights, you might offer them a small reward (tiny sticker, hug, earning points toward a bigger prize) when they report they've turned off lights. Older kids might enjoy a contest to see how many times they can catch someone else who's left a light on. Or let children make written reminders to tape by light switches: *Turn me off!*

❏ Install efficient lighting when you redecorate

If you've been looking for a good reason to redecorate your bedroom, here's one: Redecorating can help you be a better steward of the earth. Consider these lighting improvements as you make plans: Paint the room in light-reflecting colors; install lights where you need them—to read, put on make-up, or search through your closet; add daylight (skylights or windows) for daytime light; remove overhead lights or add dimmers to switches; choose fixture covers that let maximum light shine through. See the resources on page 132 for more lighting ideas.

❏ Wear warm pajamas; snuggle under insulated blankets rather than an electric blanket

Some people (arthritis sufferers, for example) may need the kind of warmth provided by an electric blanket. But if you can stay warm enough by wearing bed socks and warm pajamas, you'll save energy. This new habit can be a good reason to snuggle up to your spouse.

If you need to ease into this earth-keeping behavior, turn on the blanket to "preheat" your bed. Turn it off when you climb in, and let blankets and body heat take over for your local power plant.

❏ Choose a conventional mattress and springs rather than a waterbed that requires a heater

If you have a waterbed, you're probably spending from $10 to $30 a month to heat it. Waterbeds drain your budget and take a toll on the environment. In a year your heated waterbed could be responsible for power plants spewing into the atmosphere almost 9000 pounds of carbon dioxide, which is contributing to global warming.

If you have a waterbed and intend to keep it, avoid overfilling it. The more water you put into your waterbed, the more energy required to heat it. You can also save energy by helping your waterbed heater do its job. Put a 1-inch foam-rubber mat between the mattress and pad. Then make your bed each morning—with sheets, a cotton quilt, and a blanket—rather than leaving it unmade.

❏ Use cloth diapers whenever possible

There are 2 sides to the diaper debate. Cloth-diaper advocates contend that paper diapers consume 510,000 tons of wood pulp a year; contaminate landfills with fecal waste; make up from 1% to 4% of our solid-waste stream per year (that's about 16 billion diapers); and have plastic wrappers that will never decompose.

But paper-diaper advocates have some points too: Harvesting cotton can leave the soil open to erosion; more energy is consumed in making and cleaning cloth diapers than in making paper diapers; large amounts of bleach are used to launder diapers; diaper service trucks contribute pollutants to the atmosphere.

The vast majority of experts on this subject agree that for now the best choice is cloth diapers. They're made from a renewable resource. They don't contribute to contamination of or excess waste in our landfills. They're reusable.

Groaning parents take heart. A variety of new diapers and diaper accessories on the market make it almost as convenient to use cloth diapers as disposables—and they're much better for the earth. Check the catalog listings on page 126 for more details.

❏ **Use a washcloth and water rather than disposable paper wipes when you change your baby's diaper**

Keep a squirt bottle of water and a supply of washcloths or small, clean rags on the changing table. I have a friend who keeps her squirt bottle in an insulated container so she has warm "running" water right at hand. Going away from home? Take with you a squirt bottle and dry cloths or a container of wet cloths. Remember to put in a spare empty container for soiled cloths.

By not using disposable wipes you are saving energy, petroleum, plastic, and paper—and reducing paper and plastic waste.

Earth Keeping in Your Bedroom and Baby's Room

☐ Use cedar chips rather than mothballs.

☐ Avoid heating and cooling spare bedrooms.

☐ Sell or give away unwanted clothing.

☐ Reuse unwearable panty hose.

☐ Give excess clothes hangers to a friend or a dry cleaner who will use them.

☐ Choose natural fibers for sheets, towels, and clothing.

☐ Refuse to purchase clothing or accessories made from wild animals.

☐ Use 1 large bulb rather than 2 smaller bulbs in a multi-bulb light fixture.

☐ Turn off the light when you leave the room.

☐ Install efficient lighting when you redecorate.

☐ Wear warm pajamas; snuggle under insulated blankets rather than an electric blanket.

☐ Choose a conventional mattress and springs rather than a waterbed that requires a heater.

☐ Use cloth diapers whenever possible.

☐ Use a washcloth and water rather than disposable paper wipes when you change your baby's diaper.

You'll find a removable copy of this checklist on page 131.

6

EARTHKEEPING

in Your

Laundry Room

Yet for us there is but one God, the Father, from whom all things came and for whom we live; and there is but one Lord, Jesus Christ, through whom all things came and through whom we live.
1 CORINTHIANS 8:6

Christians, of all people, should not be the destroyers. We should treat nature with an overwhelming respect.
FRANCIS A. SCHAEFFER
POLLUTION
AND THE DEATH OF MAN

A Yale study has found that in America, the more a person participates in religious services, the less concern he or she is likely to have for nature.
MARJORIE HOPE AND JAMES
YOUNG, *CHRISTIAN*
CENTURY (AUG. 16–23, 1989)

❏ Use a phosphate-free detergent

Many detergents contain phosphates—chemical compounds that contain phosphorus. Phosphates soften water and keep dirt from redepositing on clothes. But when phosphates wash into streams, rivers, and lakes, they fertilize and cause tremendous growth in algae. When the algae eventually die, their decay uses up oxygen, robbing it from other water plants and animals. With severe phosphate contamination, all life forms in a lake or stream can die. Today phosphates are banned in more than 10 states. Even if your state allows phosphates in detergents, it's best to choose a detergent that's phosphate free.

If you have soft water, phosphate-free laundry soap (not detergent) should get your clothes clean. But don't use laundry soap in hard water; it can ruin your clothes. Instead, use a phosphate-free detergent, found right on your supermarket shelf.

The best option for cleaning laundry is a "green" cleaner. Usually available by mail order, these detergents and soaps are 100% natural, biodegradable, and phosphate-free. Check pages 126 and 130 for addresses for ordering such products. Also check page 142 for shoppers' guides for environment-friendly products of all kinds.

❏ Use less of all soaps, softeners, and cleaning products

Try cutting back on all kinds of cleaners. For instance, dilute spray-on window cleaners (or use natural cleaners instead; see pages 126, 130, and 134 for mail-order sources and recipes). Use half the amount of your regular detergent. Tear fabric softener sheets in half or thirds and use them more than once. Dilute liquid fabric softener, or try using no softener.

❏ Set your water heater at 130 degrees

Most people set their water heaters at 140 degrees. You can lower your water heater to 130 degrees and save 6% of the energy it uses at 140. The water will still be hot enough to kill bacteria, but you'll have lower energy bills and less risk of burns to children. If your heater doesn't have degree settings, look for an "energy conservation" setting or look for a suitable temperature between warm and hot.

❏ Insulate your water heater

Heating water accounts for as much as 20% of the energy used in your home. By wrapping your water heater in an insulating blanket (available at hardware stores), you can save up to 8% of the energy consumed by your heater. When you install a new water heater, choose an insulated model, which won't require an additional insulating blanket. See page 134 for other water-heater tips.

❏ Run your washer only when you have a full load

In the typical home, only toilets and showers-baths use more water than a laundry washing machine. By washing fewer loads you can easily save hundreds of gallons of water a week. Wash only full loads; combine light colors and whites to make fewer and larger loads. If you must wash a smaller load, adjust the water setting, but remember that the machine will consume the same amount of energy, whether it's washing that small load or a full load.

❏ Reduce your overall amount of laundry

Teach your family to "screen" laundry before putting it into the hamper. Look and sniff to determine if outer clothing—pants, shirts, and skirts—really need washing. If they don't, hang or fold them for another wearing. As you save water and energy, you'll also extend the life of your clothes.

❏ Wash with cold water whenever possible

When you wash clothes, more energy is consumed by heating water than by running the machine. You can save 90% of the energy used in washing by setting the dial to warm or cold water instead of hot. Experiment to see what works best for you. A cold wash is usually good enough for whites, light colors, and even most dark colors. You'll probably need a warm wash for heavily soiled loads. Since rinsing doesn't affect cleaning, you can always use cold-water rinses.

When you wash clothes in cold water, you may find it more effective to use a liquid soap or detergent. Some powdered products may not dissolve completely in cold water.

❑ Dry consecutive loads of clothes and sort clothes by weight

Take advantage of the built-up heat and warmed-up dryer parts by drying several loads of clothes consecutively. If you separate light and heavy items, you'll also save dryer time. Use a timer or your dryer's moisture sensor to avoid overdrying.

❑ Keep your dryer's lint filter and outside vent clean

A clogged lint filter or outside vent stops the flow of air inside your dryer. Consequently, the dryer has to work harder to circulate air, which in turn requires more energy.

❑ Hang clothes to dry whenever possible

How would you like to eliminate the need for 25 large power plants? The American Council for an Energy-Efficient Economy says that's what it would be like if we increased energy efficiency in our major appliances by just 10% to 30%.

The best way to make your energy-eating clothes dryer more efficient is to turn it off. String up some outdoor and indoor lines, or invest in a drying rack or a retractable clothesline. In hot weather you can dry several loads in a day. During the winter you might want to wash a full load every other day to allow for indoor drying time. Even if you use your dryer only half as often, you'll be saving 50% of the energy it would otherwise consume.

❏ Use less-toxic household cleaners whenever possible

Household cleaning products often contain chemicals that are effective cleaning agents but can harm the environment when washed down drains or deposited in landfills. Cleaning products that are less toxic may not be quite as convenient, and they may require a little more elbow grease. But while you're scrubbing, remember what part you're playing in reducing the chemical contamination of our environment. See pages 126 and 130 for inexpensive, effective, and less-toxic cleaners.

❏ Avoid using products with methyl chloroform

Methyl chloroform is used in hundreds of products such as bug sprays, fabric protectors, aerosols, spot removers, and many other cleaning products. The National Resource Defense Council states that 724 million lbs. of this ozone-depleting substance were manufactured in the U.S. in 1988. Look for products that list "1,1,1-trichloroethane" as an ingredient, and don't purchase or use them.

❏ Avoid using bleach

Chlorine's powerful bleaching action keeps on working after it goes down your drain. Heavy concentrations of bleach in bodies of water can cause deformities in marine life. The toxic effects of bleach can then travel up the food chain, as fish-eating mammals (including humans) eat contaminated fish.

Before you bleach something, try using a combination of borax and laundry soap, hanging the laundry to dry in the sun. If you must use bleach, use a dry, nonchlorine bleach— and as little as possible. I've learned to avoid unsightly, dingy dishcloths by buying colored cloths and towels, which don't need to be whitened.

❏ Avoid using your washer and dryer between 5:00 P.M. and 7:00 P.M.

Electrical plants must have the capacity to provide power during peak hours: 5:00 P.M. to 7:00 P.M. If we avoid using energy in those high-demand hours, existing power plants can meet our electrical needs—working at a steadier pace. But if consumers keep demanding energy at peak times, additional power plants will be needed. More power plants mean a greater potential for more carbon dioxide emissions.

Earth Keeping in Your Laundry Room

☐ Use a phosphate-free detergent.

☐ Use less of all soaps, softeners, and cleaning products.

☐ Set your water heater at 130 degrees.

☐ Insulate your water heater.

☐ Run your washer only when you have a full load.

☐ Reduce your overall amount of laundry.

☐ Wash with cold water whenever possible.

☐ Dry consecutive loads of clothes and sort clothes by weight.

☐ Keep your dryer's lint filter and outside vent clean.

☐ Hang clothes to dry whenever possible.

☐ Use less-toxic household cleaners whenever possible.

☐ Avoid using products with methyl chloroform

☐ Avoid using bleach.

☐ Avoid using your washer and dryer between 5:00 P.M. and 7:00 P.M.

You'll find a removable copy of this checklist on page 133.

7

EARTEEPING

in Your

Garage and Workshop

Then I was the craftsman at his side.
I was filled with delight day after day,
   rejoicing always in his presence,
rejoicing in his whole world
   and delighting in mankind.
                              PROVERBS 8:30–31

The reality that we are dealing with is much more serious than the destruction of an artist's creation. These are creations of our Creator. This is our Lord's earth!
                              CALVIN DEWITT, QUOTED IN
                              MOODY MONTHLY (OCT. 1989)

Only a monumental effort can reverse the deterioration of the planet.
                              LESTER R. BROWN
                              STATE OF THE WORLD 1990

❑ Use latex, not oil-based, paint

You, like me, might put off your painting jobs as long as possible. But other Americans used 3 million gallons of paint today—and every day all year. When you finally start painting, be sure to avoid oil-based paint; its pigments and solvents contain toxic chemicals. The paint itself is dangerous to the environment, and the manufacturing process produces dangerous by-products.

Choose latex or natural paint. Latex paint is water-based and comes in glossy and flat finishes that are long-lasting and washable. Natural paints have citric or linseed oil bases and can be tinted with nontoxic mineral pigments. Natural paints can be hard to find; check page 136 for sources.

❏ Clean paintbrushes and dispose of paint safely

If you have leftover oil-based paint that you want to dispose of (and that's the best thing to do with it), there is only one safe and lawful way to get rid of it: Take it to a hazardous waste disposal site. Don't put it into your regular trash. The same is true for paint thinner left over from cleaning your brushes.

Latex paint can be discarded with your regular trash. But why throw away something someone else can use? Try giving away leftover latex paint or selling it at a garage sale. Wash paintbrushes soiled with latex paint in your sink (where it will go into your city's sewer system), not outside with a bucket or hose (where its chemicals can contaminate ground-water).

❏ Store and dispose of hazardous materials properly

Are you wondering just what constitutes hazardous waste? The list includes almost all household cleaners and disinfec-tants; any fluids, oils, or gases used in your automobile; any glues or cleaners containing solvents; all paints, paint thinners, varnishes, paint strippers, and wood preservatives; all pesticides and herbicides; batteries, chemicals, mothballs, acids, and ammunition. See page 136 for additional items.

How should you dispose of hazardous wastes? It depends. Some may be poured down your drain with plenty of water; some may go to the landfill with your regular trash; some are recyclable (including automobile fluids and oils); some must be taken to a hazardous-waste site.

How do you know which should go where? You can probably obtain a detailed guide from your local recycling center. To be cautious, you might treat any product marked *caution, toxic, danger, warning, flammable, poisonous, reactive,* or *explosive* as hazardous waste and take it to a hazardous-waste collection center.

While waiting to dispose of hazardous wastes, be sure to keep them in the original containers, tightly closed, and out of reach of children and pets.

❏ Avoid buying halon fire extinguishers

Halons are bromine-containing chemicals developed to fight fires in places (such as computer work stations, libraries, museums, and electronic centers) where water would cause extensive damage. Halons have recently been introduced in home fire extinguishers. Unfortunately, like chlorofluorocarbons, halons damage our ozone layer.

If you have a halon fire extinguisher, dispose of it with hazardous waste. When you buy a new fire extinguisher, make sure it does not contain halons.

❏ Buy workshop supplies (nails, screws, etc.) in bulk, then store them in reusable kitchen containers (yogurt cups, baby food jars, cans with lids)

Here's a great opportunity to precycle and reuse. Precycle by choosing supplies that come without packages. Reuse food containers from the kitchen to hold the items you bought in bulk.

❑ **When you clean out your garage, have a garage sale or give away unwanted items**

Reduce, reuse, recycle. That's what garage sales are all about. If your sale doesn't get rid of everything you've cleaned out from the house and garage, give the rest away. Some organizations, including AmVets, will pick up what's left, saving you the trouble of hauling it away.

❑ **Use castor oil or mineral oil to lubricate squeaky hinges, reluctant locks, stiff doorknobs, and noisy garage doors**

Instead of using aerosol sprays that contain ozone-damaging pollutants, squirt or drip castor oil or mineral oil on those squeaky culprits. Avoid using salad oil, which over time can develop a rancid smell.

❑ **Check for leaks in faucets and toilets and repair them as soon as you can**

Whoever is in charge of the workshop is probably in charge of leaky faucets. If it's you, be sure to catch those drips as soon as possible because even a tiny drip can waste 50 gallons of water a day.

Also check the toilet to see if water is leaking from the tank into the bowl. Put a few drops of food coloring into the tank water. If you have a leak, you'll see colored water in the bowl within a few minutes. You may be able to repair the tank ball or valve and stop the leak. Or you may need to purchase a new toilet. (If you do, choose a water-saving model.)

❑ Use a battery recharger and rechargeable batteries

Americans use 2 billion disposable batteries every year. And most of them end up in our landfills, where they corrode, leak, and break apart, releasing toxic heavy metals such as mercury and cadmium. If the batteries are burned with other trash, they release these same dangerous chemicals into the air.

Rechargeable batteries contain cadmium, but they reduce battery use and waste because they last much longer than alkaline batteries. Until you buy a recharger, recycle your used alkaline or other batteries—if a battery recycling service is available in your area. If not, dispose of these batteries with hazardous waste.

A tip to precyclers: Before you buy a battery-operated product, make sure it will work with rechargeable batteries.

❑ Check yearly for leaks around windows and doors; caulk and weatherstrip as needed

You can schedule a professional energy audit for your home, or you can easily check for air leaks around windows and doors yourself. Slowly move a lighted candle in front of window and door frames and sashes. (Be careful around curtains, drapes, and other flammable materials.) If the candle flame flickers in a draft, you have a leak and a good reason to weatherproof that location.

To weatherproof your home, you'll need caulking supplies and weather stripping. You can also buy insulators to install behind electrical switch-plates and outlets, as well as "sweeps" or "shoes" to add to the bottoms of outside doors. Be sure to cover outdoor-mounted window air conditioners as well as ventilating fans that keep your home cool in the summer.

You may have to spend some money to weatherproof your home, but you'll make up for it in saved energy costs. If every home in our country with gas heat were properly weather-proofed, an estimated 4 million homes could be heated with the natural gas we would save.

❏ Install storm or other insulating-type windows

Every day the energy equivalent of 1.8 million barrels of oil—the daily flow through the Alaska pipeline—flows out our windows in the form of lost heat and air conditioning. Insulated windows can reduce your heating and cooling energy consumption by up to 15% a year. That means you can save an annual 10 to 15 dollars per window. Storm doors could reduce your annual energy bill by $170.

If you can, install combination storm-and-screen windows. They're good insulators, and they give you easy access to fresh air when you don't need heat or air conditioning. Double-pane windows are also good insulators. Simpler and less expensive options include attaching plastic sheets or film to your window surfaces.

Watch for new windows on the market. First available in 1981, low-E (emissivity) windows are comparable to an inch of foam insulation and insulate 4 times better than single-pane glass. Other prototype windows, called superwindows, can insulate up to 12 times better than the standard. These windows may soon be competitively priced.

❏ Insulate your walls and attic

Insulating your house can help combat one of the leading causes of household energy waste. Attic and wall insulation can save you an incredible 4 months' worth of household energy every year. Though a sizable investment to install, insulation can easily pay for itself in reduced energy bills.

If you plan to insulate your home yourself, you'll need an understanding of "R-values" to buy the right kind of insulation. Ask at your hardware store or consult with your local utility company to choose the appropriate type of insulation. Whatever you choose, avoid rigid-foam insulation. It contains chlorofluorocarbons that damage the ozone layer.

If expense or time requires you to install insulation in stages, begin with attic insulation. In most cases, it will achieve the most dramatic effect.

Note to insulation installers: There is increasing concern about insulating a building to the point of cutting off adequate ventilation, which could increase indoor pollution. See page 132 for more about how to avoid this problem.

Earth Keeping in Your Garage and Workshop

☐ Use latex, not oil-based, paint.

☐ Clean paintbrushes and dispose of paint safely.

☐ Store and dispose of hazardous materials properly.

☐ Avoid buying halon fire extinguishers.

☐ Buy workshop supplies (nails, screws, etc.) in bulk, then store them in reusable kitchen containers (yogurt cups, baby food jars, cans with lids).

☐ When you clean out your garage, have a garage sale or give away unwanted items.

☐ Use castor oil or mineral oil to lubricate squeaky hinges, reluctant locks, stiff doorknobs, and noisy garage doors.

☐ Check for leaks in faucets and toilets and repair them as soon as you can.

☐ Use a battery recharger and rechargeable batteries.

☐ Check yearly for leaks around windows and doors; caulk and weatherstrip as needed.

☐ Install storm or other insulating-type windows.

☐ Insulate your walls and attic.

You'll find a removable copy of this checklist on page 135.

8
EARTHKEEPING

in Your

Yard

The Lord God took the man and put him in the Garden of Eden to work it and take care of it.
GENESIS 2:15

We could stand side by side, Adam and I, he in his skin shirt and I in my grubby jeans, hoeing, stopping to tear out an upstart cocklebur, pausing to lean on the hoe handle while we stare out at the horizon . . . Adam and Adam's child, cursed and blessed from the same ground.
VIRGINIA STEM OWENS .
CHRISTIANITY TODAY
(DEC. 17, 1976)

We abuse land because we regard it as a commodity belonging to us. When we see land as a community to which we belong, we may begin to use it with love and respect.
ALDO LEOPOLD
A SAND COUNTY ALMANAC

❏ Clean driveways, walks, and patios with a broom

Americans use 2 to 4 times as much water as people in European countries. You can save hundreds of gallons of water just by changing one cleaning habit: Sweep rather than wash your outdoor areas.

Water can gush out of your garden hose as fast as 20 gallons a minute. Every time you wash down outdoor areas rather than sweep them, you waste hundreds of gallons of water. By sweeping, you immediately cut all that water waste to zero.

67

❏ Avoid using lighter fluid to light coals for outdoor cooking

Cooking on an outdoor barbecue causes air pollution, no matter what you do. But you can reduce the emission of damaging gases by lighting the coals with kindling or newspaper, rather than lighter fluid. Check the mail order catalogs on page 126 for outdoor cooking accessories that can help you heat coals quickly and efficiently.

Charcoal and gas grilling also create cancer-causing benzo(a)pyrene. To reduce the risk of ingesting benzo(a)pyrene, cook the meat as far away from the heat or flame as possible; choose lean rather than fatty meat, and keep cooking time to a minimum.

❏ Attract wild birds to your yard

Making your yard appealing to wild birds can help you and them. By providing homes, food, and safe places to live, we can give back a little of the habitat we've taken away from the natural inhabitants of our living space. In return, we get a close encounter with nature and some helpful insect eaters.

In all seasons keep fresh water in a bird bath. (Many animals have difficulty finding fresh water in freezing weather.) Bird houses, bird seed, and plants with colorful flowers, seeds, and fruit will also attract birds. See page 138 for resources on turning your yard into a haven for helpful wildlife.

❏ Water deeply in mornings or evenings

Water probably came out of your tap when you turned it on today, but that doesn't mean it always will. In many countries indoor taps sit dry and useless while residents line up at community spigots for a few gallons of water a day. Could that ever happen here? It's not as unlikely as you might think.

In the U.S. 96% of our fresh water is from underground streams and reservoirs, called aquifers. In fact, aquifers hold almost 50 times as much water as the lakes and rivers on our planet.

In recent history, our water demands have put great stress on our groundwater supply. The vast Ogalala Aquifer, stretching under the Great Plains, for example, could be drained dry within 40 years. If for no other reason than self-preservation, we must conserve water.

Water your lawn during the cooler times of day: early morning or in the evening. Water slowly and long enough for the water to seep down to where it's needed most—at the plants' roots. If you water deeply and infrequently, you encourage deep rooting in your plants, making them more drought-tolerant. Light, surface sprinkling encourages shallow root growth and allows water to evaporate.

❏ Keep your mower blades sharp and set them high

Keeping mower blades sharp helps protect the health of your plants. Dull blades tug at the grass plants and weaken their roots. Sharp blades cut cleanly and leave your lawn stronger and healthier.

By setting your mower blades at a height of 2 or 3 inches, you leave your grass long enough to provide shade for its own roots. And that helps the soil retain moisture longer. If you water your lawn regularly, a longer lawn can help you water less. By stretching the number of days between waterings, you can save from 500 to 1,500 gallons of water every month.

❏ **Take plastic pots and trays back to your local plant nursery**

Many nurseries now accept used plant pots and trays for reuse. Some even give you money back or credit toward a purchase for the returned containers. Every time you make a used container available for reuse, you save 100% of the energy and materials required to make a new container.

❏ **Landscape with low-maintenance, drought-tolerant plants**

A wide variety of plants take less upkeep—time and water—than a lawn. If you have a grass lawn and can relandscape, carefully consider the kinds of plants you choose. Contact your local nursery for lists of plants that do well with little water. You might be pleasantly surprised at the variety of available species—including species native to your locale.

❏ **Plant trees, shrubs, and other leafy plants rather than large lawns**

Due to the loss of tropical forests and the pollution caused by automobiles and power plants, our atmosphere holds a tremendous excess of carbon dioxide. Plants with vigorous leafing patterns absorb carbon dioxide efficiently and put oxygen back into the air better than other plants. Instead of planting a lawn, choose trees, leafy shrubs, and other leafy plants that grow well in your area.

❏ **Use grass clippings for mulch and/or compost**

Yard waste makes up about 20% of all landfill waste. A good part of that yard waste is grass clippings, which can go to good use—fertilizing your lawn and helping it retain water.

Why not leave the clippings right where they fall? If your lawn is chemical-free, the clippings will begin to decompose right away; they can provide up to half the nitrogen your lawn needs. You might also rake up the clippings to use as mulch in your garden, or put them into your compost pile.

Under some circumstances you should not leave clippings on your lawn: when you're converting from a chemical to an organic system; after the first spring mowing; after the last fall mowing; and whenever you mow more than half the top growth.

If you can't make use of your grass clippings, check around to see if someone else can. In our city for a fee you can unload yard waste at a greenery section of the landfill. The waste is composted into mulch used in city parks and landfills and made available to city residents for free. Some private businesses offer a similar service.

❑ Build and use a compost pile

If you're not doing this already, it probably sounds like a lot of work. If you are doing it, you're probably surprised at how little work it takes.

The environmental payoff for composting is a big one. Right now, up to 70% of our kitchen and yard waste is compostable. If everyone in the United States composted, we could reduce our cities' landfill loads by 40%. Another benefit is the natural by-product of composting: rich fertilizer for lawns and gardens.

Composting is as simple as piling leaves and grass clippings in a corner of your yard, or as complex as developing a city-wide composting program. The basic idea is to layer organic waste (that is, trimmings and leftovers from produce, grass clippings, leaves) with dirt, sprinkle with water, and turn or mix periodically. The resulting mixture is a dark, rich, earthy-smelling soil conditioner. If you want to get started or simply want to learn more about it, check the resources and the mail-order companies on page 138.

A word of caution: If you have used chemical fertilizers and pesticides in your yard, it's best to switch to organic products, then wait a few weeks before composting the yard waste. You'll avoid adding toxic chemicals to the compost and, later, to your soil.

❏ Control pests naturally and use organic fertilizer

Pests are aptly named, aren't they? And getting rid of them isn't always easy. There are the obvious earth-friendly deterrents: keeping your yard and home free of debris and garbage; using the hose to wash away insects; putting nets over food plants; even picking off bugs by hand. But if those don't work, you may need more help.

You can take 2 steps before you turn to the chemical pesticides so readily available in stores. You might try various home remedies, like circling plants with diatomaceous earth (make sure it's not chemically treated) to protect against cutworms, trapping snails by providing a board for them to crawl under for shade, or scattering seeds or corn for birds near pest-infested plants. If home remedies don't work, consider natural pesticides, generally less toxic and with shorter-lived negative effects than chemical pesticides. See page 138 for resources for purchasing natural pesticides.

On labels watch for warning words. Here's what they mean on pesticides: DANGER = highly toxic; WARNING = moderately toxic; CAUTION = slightly toxic.

Choosing nonchemical fertilizers for your lawn and garden helps prevent toxic chemicals from washing into our water supplies. Look for commercial brands of organic fertilizers (including Fertrell, Erth-Rite, and Ringer's Lawn Restore) or check page 138 for mail-order natural fertilizers. Whatever product you choose, be sure to follow the directions carefully.

If you use a lawn service, find out what kinds of pesticides and fertilizers your gardeners use. Thousands of companies use millions of pounds of pesticides on our lawns every year.

❑ Plant a garden

When you choose to put part of your yard into a garden, you help the environment in several ways: by reducing the amount of your water-consuming (and "unproductive") lawn; by producing home-grown, edible produce that doesn't have to be shipped in to you; by enriching your soil. Then there's the pleasure derived from working close to nature.

Before planting your garden, take some time to plan it. Consider planting species that help protect each other from pests. Learn about drip irrigation. Find out how to grow food and flowers organically. See page 138 for gardening resources that can help you plan well.

❑ Water with soaker hoses or drip irrigation wherever possible

Rubber soaker hoses slowly leak water into the soil, allowing your garden or shrubs to absorb more deeply, which means you water less often. With this method all the water gets delivered to the ground; none shoots into the air, where it evaporates. Though a drip irrigation system may be more costly to purchase and install, you'll likely find it more

convenient after it's in. And it can be 50% more efficient than
watering with a sprinkler.

❏ Plant shade trees near your house

Deciduous (not evergreen) shade trees on the southeast and
southwest sides of a home can save 10% to 15% on cooling
costs in the summer. In the winter these leafless trees allow
the warming sunlight through. As you plant your own trees,
encourage your neighbors to plant. Studies show that city
neighborhoods thickly planted with trees can be up to 9
degrees cooler in hot weather than sparsely planted neighborhoods.

You might make a family project of planting trees—in honor
of your children or their grandparents or . . .

Consider becoming involved in one of several global greening
campaigns. Widespread tree planting can help our environment in many ways, including cooling cities, battling the
greenhouse effect, preventing erosion, providing food, and
reducing energy needs. See page 140 for more information.

Earth Keeping in Your Yard

❑ Clean driveways, walks, and patios with a broom.

❑ Avoid using lighter fluid to light coals for outdoor cooking.

❑ Attract wild birds to your yard.

❑ Water deeply in mornings or evenings.

❑ Keep your mower blades sharp and set them high.

❑ Take plastic pots and trays back to your local plant nursery.

❑ Landscape with low-maintenance, drought-tolerant plants.

❑ Plant trees, shrubs, and other leafy plants rather than large lawns.

❑ Use grass clippings for mulch and/or compost.

❑ Build and use a compost pile.

❑ Control pests naturally and use organic fertilizer.

❑ Plant a garden.

❑ Water with soaker hoses or drip irrigation wherever possible.

❑ Plant shade trees near your house.

You'll find a removable copy of this checklist on page 137.

9

EARTHKEEPING

in Your

Car

> Trust in the Lord with all your heart
>> and lean not on your own understanding;
> in all your ways acknowledge him,
>> and he will make your paths straight.
>
> PROVERBS 3:5–6

> The church is being called to the forgotten task of saving the earth.
> Christians everywhere who hear this call can now find specific,
> practical avenues for living it out.
>
> WESLEY GRANBERG-MICHAELSON
> *ECOLOGY AND LIFE*

> Driving a fuel-efficient car may be the simplest and most immedi-
> ate step you can take to help stop global warming and reduce acid
> rain.
>
> DIANE MACEACHERN
> *SAVE OUR PLANET*

❏ **If your car idles more than a minute, turn it off**

Idling just 30 seconds can consume more gas than starting
up your engine. If you stop to pick up a friend or wait while
someone runs into a store, turn off your car. Ordinarily you
wouldn't turn off the ignition in traffic, but you might
consider it if stopped at length. Also avoid warming up your
car any longer than necessary.

❏ Use a trigger nozzle and bucket when washing your car

An automatic car wash can use 10 times the water you would use at home. Even if the car wash recycles that water, the equipment also consumes a great deal of electricity, while a home-wash requires none.

When washing your car at home, hose it down, then scrub with a sponge and bucket. Use a trigger-nozzle hose that turns off the water when you're not rinsing the car. Another alternative is a self-service car wash, which uses 10 to 15 gallons of water—approximately one-tenth the amount used at an automatic car wash.

❏ Avoid topping off your gas tank

There are several good reasons to stop filling your car's tank after the first or second click from the nozzle's automatic shut-off: Overflowing gas wastes money, can be a fire hazard, can damage your car's paint, and contributes to pollution.

Butane vapors of evaporating gasoline pollute the air. That's the reason for plastic hoods on gas pump handles. (Don't pull them back.)

❏ Use unleaded gasoline if possible

If your car requires unleaded gas, use it. Surveys indicate that as many as 14% of the drivers in the United States use leaded gas when they should be using unleaded. This fuel switching increases automotive emissions, pumping hydrocarbons, nitrogen oxide, and lead into the atmosphere. These materials increase global warming and acid rain and contribute to serious health problems.

❑ Drive smoothly: Speed up and slow down gradually; avoid tailgating; don't exceed 55 miles per hour

Frequent or unnecessary starting, stopping, slowing down, and speeding up, as well as quick stops and jack-rabbit starts, use extra fuel. The most fuel-efficient way to drive is steadily, stopping the forward motion of your car as gently and infrequently as possible. Tailgating, besides being dangerous, requires you to stop and start constantly, wasting fuel.

Driving above speed limits on the highway also reduces fuel economy. The faster you go, the more wind resistance your car encounters. Driving at 70 miles per hour can reduce your fuel efficiency by 20% to 30%. Your car uses fuel most efficiently at speeds of 50 to 55 miles per hour.

❑ Plan your trips carefully: Combine errands, plan your route, and call ahead

In 1990 Americans drove more than 3 trillion miles. If experts' estimates hold true, we could be driving 6 trillion miles a year by 2010. These figures show that global warming, caused in part by carbon dioxide emissions from cars, will get dramatically worse if we don't change our driving behaviors.

Oil companies, researchers, and engineers are working on options to today's gasoline. Until 1 or more of these options—including "clean" gas, ethanol, compressed natural gas, methanol, electricity, and solar-hydrogen fuel—become viable on a large scale, we drivers have to do something about our gas-guzzling habits.

Smart driving starts with smart planning—before you ever get into your car. Be sure of your route; consolidate errands; call ahead to verify store hours. Ask a basic question: Is this trip necessary?

❏ Carpool whenever possible—to work, church, and social events

Consumer Reports says that Americans will drive 25 billion more miles this year than last year. To personalize that statistic, another source states that the average U.S. driver will spend about 45 8-hour days behind the wheel of a car this year. Carpooling is probably the single biggest step you can take to reduce the miles you drive.

You might start this habit, like many others, gradually. Try to carpool to work 1 day a week, or carpool the kids to school 2 or 3 days. Ask if you can work 4 10-hour days. If you have a minivan or station wagon, fill up the extra seats with neighbors and friends when you go to church or social activities. Look for opportunities to share rides with others.

❏ Drive less. Bike, walk, and use public transportation more

Each year an average car releases about 5 tons of carbon dioxide into the atmosphere. That means America's 127 million cars together contribute more than 600 million tons of carbon dioxide a year. So every time you decide not to use your car, you help combat global warming.

It's especially helpful to reduce or eliminate those short car trips you often make. Instead of driving a half-mile for milk or a newspaper, try walking or bicycling. Does it feel as if you're going to a lot of trouble for nothing? Be assured that your time and trouble pay off; your car burns more than twice as much gasoline during the first few warm-up minutes than at other times.

❑ Avoid drive-through lines and rush-hour traffic

Your car consumes about a gallon of gas for every 1 to 2 hours it idles. Americans stuck in rush-hour traffic waste about 3 billion gallons of gas every year. Whenever you can, plan alternate routes or times to avoid rush-hour traffic. When you stop at the bank or a fast-food restaurant, park and go inside rather than wait in a drive-through line.

❑ Keep your car's air conditioner in good repair; choose a service station that captures and recycles air-conditioner refrigerant

The air conditioners in an estimated 95 million American cars are a major source of chlorofluorocarbon (CFC) emissions that are destroying our ozone layer. If your car has an air conditioner, keep it in good repair and have it checked regularly for leaks. CFCs can leak into the atmosphere from many places in a car's air-conditioning system, including hoses, seals, and gaskets. If your car's air conditioner needs repair, make sure the technician captures the CFCs with special equipment (variously called "vampire," "emission control," or "vapor recovery"), then recycles them. Never recharge your car's air conditioner without first having it repaired. If you do, the replacement refrigerant will leak out too, compounding the damage to the environment.

Stay on the alert for alternatives to CFC refrigerants. General Motors has already announced their intention to phase out CFCs in their car air conditioners by 1994. If you buy a car in the near future, consider getting one without air conditioning. By not purchasing air conditioning you will reduce CFC damage to our ozone layer, and you can save more than a gallon of gas for each tankful consumed by your car.

❏ Properly inflate, balance, and rotate your tires

If underinflated, tires cause "drag," which can increase a car's fuel consumption by as much as 6%. Between 50% and 80% of the half-billion tires rolling our roads are underinflated. If these car owners properly inflated their tires, we could save 2 billion gallons of gas per year. Properly inflated, balanced, and rotated tires also last longer—making better use of the resources that go into making the tires.

❏ Use radial tires, especially steel-belted radials

- Radial tires, especially steel-belted, are constructed to grip the road more efficiently than other tires. Consequently, radial tires can increase your gas mileage by about 1 mile per gallon.

❏ Choose service stations that recycle brake fluid, oil, batteries, tires, and air conditioner refrigerant

This earth-keeping behavior may take a number of phone calls and some extra trouble, but it can go a long way toward helping our environment. More and more car dealerships and service stations are recycling automobile fluids, including oil, brake fluid, and antifreeze. If you service your own car, look for automotive centers that will clean your car's fluids so you can reuse them. Some service stations will buy back car batteries, then reuse the lead in making new batteries.

You may not be aware of it, but about 80% of car batteries in the U.S. are recycled each year. Discarded batteries are sent to factories where their lead, sulfuric acid, and plastic are separated and reused, recycled, or disposed of safely (in the case of some sulfuric acid). When it's time to replace your car's battery, buy one from a store that will recycle your old one.

When you buy new tires, try to find a tire dealer who recycles old tires, or at least turns them over to a licensed carter. Right now there are about 3 billion tires resting in landfills or illegal dumping sites across the U.S. They take up precious landfill space and pose tremendous fire hazards. Hopefully future markets will be found for scrap rubber. Until then, get the most wear you can from your tires and recycle old ones if possible.

Leaky car air conditioners are a main source of the chloro-fluorocarbons that are damaging our ozone layer. So when your car's air conditioner breaks down, have it fixed immediately. When it's serviced, make sure your service station captures and recycles the refrigerant. Refrigerant on the loose releases ozone-damaging gases into the atmosphere.

❏ Service your car regularly; keep all filters clean

A car tuned up every 5000 to 10,000 miles has a longer life and uses as much as 9% less gasoline than a poorly tuned car.

❏ When you buy a car, choose a fuel-efficient model

Let's say your present car gets 26 miles per gallon; over its life it will emit almost 40 tons of carbon dioxide into the atmosphere. If your next car gets 45 miles per gallon, the carbon dioxide emissions will drop to about 25 tons. Cars that get 60 miles per gallon (Geo Metro now gets 58 miles per gallon on the highway) will emit only about 17 tons. So when buying a car, choose the most fuel-efficient model you can. You'll feel the difference in your wallet when you fill up the tank, and as soon as the majority of motorists buy fuel-efficient cars, we'll all breathe a little easier.

Earth Keeping in Your Car

☐ If your car idles more than a minute, turn it off.

☐ Use a trigger nozzle and bucket when washing your car.

☐ Avoid topping off your gas tank.

☐ Use unleaded gasoline if possible.

☐ Drive smoothly: Speed up and slow down gradually. Avoid tailgating. Don't exceed 55 miles per hour.

☐ Plan your trips carefully: Combine errands. Plan your route. Call ahead.

☐ Carpool whenever possible—to work, church, and social events.

☐ Drive less. Bike, walk, and use public transportation more.

☐ Avoid drive-through lines and rush-hour traffic.

☐ Keep your car's air conditioner in good repair; choose a service station that captures and recycles air conditioner refrigerant.

☐ Properly inflate, balance, and rotate your tires.

☐ Use radial tires, especially steel-belted radials.

☐ Choose service stations that recycle brake fluid, oil, batteries, tires, and air conditioner refrigerant.

☐ Service your car regularly. Keep all filters clean.

☐ When you buy a car, choose a fuel-efficient model.

You'll find a removable copy of this checklist on page 139.

10
EARTHKEEPING

at the
Grocery Store

Follow my decrees and be careful to obey my laws, and you will live safely in the land. Then the land will yield its fruit, and you will eat your fill and live there in safety.
LEVITICUS 25:18–19

Man is placed in the world by God to be its lord. . . . As soon as he begins to use it selfishly, and reaches out to take the fruit which is forbidden by the Lord, instantly the ecological balance is upset and nature begins to groan.
C. F. D. MOULE
MAN AND NATURE IN THE
NEW TESTAMENT

You probably don't realize it, but every week you make dozens of decisions that directly affect the environment of the planet Earth. . . . But the products and services you buy need not be so destructive to the environment.
JOHN ELKINGTON, JULIA HAILES,
JOEL MAKOWER
THE GREEN CONSUMER

❏ Refuse to buy products packaged in polystyrene foam (Styrofoam)

It's easy to understand why we see polystyrene foam products everywhere: They're good insulators, lightweight, and inexpensive to produce. But the reasons why you should stop using polystyrene foam far outweigh its positive points: Being petroleum-based, it uses up our limited supply of oil; not being degradable, it will sit in our landfills and float in our oceans forever; containing a lot of air, it takes up even

85

more than its share of landfill space; looking like crumbs of food, pieces of foam are eaten by marine animals, often resulting in their deaths. Besides all that, manufacture of the foam releases ozone-damaging chlorofluorocarbons (CFCs) and other smog-producing gases.

At the store, avoid polystyrene foam in disposable cups and plates and all kinds of packaging, including meat trays and egg cartons. Carry this habit with you outside the store and refuse to buy fast-food items packaged in plastic foam. Pad mail packages with newspaper, not foam pellets.

If polystyrene foam recycling is available to you, by all means take advantage of it. But even then, severely limit or eliminate your use of this material.

❏ If you don't need a bag, don't take one

We've become conditioned to think we need to place each kind of produce we buy into its own plastic or paper bag. We really don't. Why not put your produce loose into your shopping basket? Now that my children no longer ride in the basket, I put loose produce in that upper "seat." You might take smaller cloth, mesh, or string bags to the store. But if you forget, stop your hand in midair as you reach for one of those bags. By choosing not to take a plastic or paper bag, you've just avoided using a product that consumes resources unnecessarily.

❏ Leave the plastic bag fasteners at the store

No need to dwell on this one, especially since you're not using plastic bags anymore, right? Pat yourself on the back as you stroll your produce past these little resource-wasters.

❏ Take your own paper, cloth, or string bags to the store

This new habit will take some getting used to. You'll have to plan ahead, and you may need to buy or make some reusable bags. Using bags provided by the store is not an earth-friendly option, even though we've done it that way for as long as I can remember. The problem is with the choices: Paper or plastic—each is an extravagant waste of resources.

The one good thing about paper bags is that they're biodegradable. But we know that even paper doesn't readily degrade in our landfills. And paper bags, though they're recyclable, are not made from recycled materials. That's because the long fibers contained in virgin pulp (direct from trees) are required to make the bags stronger.

Plastic bags have two main deficiencies: They are not biodegradable, and they are petroleum-based. Take advantage of the new plastic bag recycling bins available in many stores, but avoid acquiring additional plastic bags.

You don't have to buy special cloth bags for your groceries and other purchases. At garage sales you can pick up straw or cloth bags at a good price, or you can make your own. See the resources listed on page 126 for mail-order shopping bags.

❏ Keep extra shopping bags in your car

Now here's a dilemma: You're out in your car, consolidating errands. But you forgot to bring your own bags for a quick run into a store. Do you waste gas driving home to get the bags? Or do you accept the store's paper or plastic bags and use unnecessary resources?

I frequently faced this dilemma when I began using my own bags, until I started to carry the solution right with me. Now I keep shopping bags in the car. Why not put the bags right back into the car after you've unloaded your groceries? That takes care of their storage, and they're right where you need them for your next shopping trip.

❏ Choose products with the least packaging

This easy habit can go a long way toward conserving natural resources; 50% of all the paper, 90% of all the glass, and 11% of all the aluminum produced in the U.S. are used in product packaging.

So, while you're standing in the store aisle trying to decide which brand to take off the shelf, consider the packaging element. The product with the least packaging could be the best choice for the environment.

❏ Choose products sold in recycled or recyclable packaging

Packaging makes up 50% of the volume and 30% of the weight of the tremendous stream of waste that flows from our cities. Look for products that are in recyclable paper, glass, or aluminum. (Plastic is less preferable, as it is more difficult to recycle.) Then remember to recycle the package.

❏ Buy in bulk whenever possible

The best choice in packaging, of course, is no package at all. Pull out one of the bags you brought to the store and fill it up at bulk-food bins. Also choose loose, not prepackaged, produce.

❑ Buy the largest package possible

You're probably starting to get the drift by now: the less package, the better. That's why you look for shampoo, vinegar, and ketchup in huge (preferably glass) bottles. There's more product and less package. You can keep smaller containers at home to fill from these large ones. And larger sizes are usually a better buy too.

If you have room to store larger amounts of products you constantly use, you can add another savings to your environmental score card: Each time you avoid a trip to the store, you're saving energy and keeping some carbon dioxide out of the atmosphere.

❑ Be aware of environment-friendly products of all kinds and buy those brands

Apply what you know about products and packaging to decisions you make at the store. Add to what you know by keeping up on current environmental and stewardship topics, such as the destruction of America's old-growth forests and dolphin-safe tuna. Check page 142 for shoppers' guides to help you identify earth-friendly products.

Whenever your children or spouse accompany you on shopping trips, it's a great opportunity to explain the environmental reasons behind your choices. Point out why you pass over a particular brand because it's packaged in plastic; explain why you buy rice or beans in bulk; let a child locate a brand of paper towels made from recycled paper. Children (especially) catch on quickly. I've overheard my own children explaining to their friends why they didn't choose particular products because of their packaging.

❏ Read labels before you buy

In an effort to keep toxic chemicals out of our water, ground, and atmosphere, read labels carefully to determine exactly what's in the product. Be suspicious of products that don't list ingredients. Stay away from products that imply warning or danger.

❏ Avoid buying products that contain chlorofluorocarbons (CFCs)

Chlorofluorocarbons were once thought to be harmless nontoxic chemicals. But now we know they cause severe atmospheric damage. When released into the air, CFCs float up to the stratosphere, where they're exposed to ultraviolet rays which react with the CFCs to release chlorine. Chlorine in turn destroys an atmospheric component called ozone. When the ozone layer thins or breaks apart, the sun's harmful rays can pass through to the earth's surface. As we become exposed to more and more radiation, we risk the increase of infectious diseases, cancer, and immune-system disorders.

When you shop, avoid all products containing:

- CFC-11 (trichlorofluoromethane);
- CFC-12 (dichlorodifluoromethane);
- CFC-113 (trichlorotrifluoroethane);
- CFC-114 (dichlorotetrafluoroethane);
- CFC-115 (monochloropentafluoroethane).

These harmful CFCs are found mostly in a few aerosol products, spray cans of confetti, and various cleaning sprays for electronic equipment.

❏ Buy organic, locally grown foods in season

Produce grown close to its retail outlet is more likely to be organically grown—free of chemical pesticides and fertilizers. It is usually fresher and often cheaper. In addition, by buying locally grown produce in season, you support a product that has not consumed large amounts of energy in transport.

❏ Buy unbleached products whenever possible.

The process that whitens paper pulp also releases dioxins, a group of toxic, carcinogenic chemicals that include agent orange and TCDD—the most toxic substance ever made. Dioxins washed into waterways and oceans have catastrophic effects on aquatic life. But not all dioxins are washed out of the product. Some remain behind in products that can contaminate food—such as bleached milk cartons and coffee filters.

Dioxin pollution off the coast of Sweden has harmed the sea life and prompted Swedish consumers to purchase non-bleached instead of bleached products. Could you get used to the tan-colored toilet paper, milk cartons, tampons, and coffee filters that are stocked on Swedish shelves? It's all in the eyes of the beholder: Swedish consumers now think of whiteness as indicative of pollution, not purity.

Industries are developing new, safer ways to whiten paper pulp. In the meantime, it's best to avoid bleached products whenever you can. Purchase unbleached or permanent coffee filters; look for unbleached toilet paper; use recycled paper (that bleaching process doesn't usually use dioxins). Check page 126 for companies that provide unbleached products by mail.

Earth Keeping at the Grocery Store

❑ Refuse to buy products packaged in polystyrene foam (Styrofoam).

❑ If you don't need a bag, don't take one.

❑ Leave the plastic bag fasteners at the store.

❑ Take your own paper, cloth, or string bags to the store.

❑ Keep extra shopping bags in your car.

❑ Choose products with the least packaging.

❑ Choose products sold in recycled or recyclable packaging.

❑ Buy in bulk whenever possible.

❑ Buy the largest package possible.

❑ Be aware of environment-friendly products of all kinds and buy those brands.

❑ Read labels before you buy.

❑ Avoid buying products that contain chlorofluorocarbons (CFCs).

❑ Buy organic, locally grown foods in season.

❑ Buy unbleached products whenever possible.

You'll find a removable copy of this checklist on page 141.

11

EARTHKEEPING

with Your
Influence

The law of the Lord is perfect,
  reviving the soul.
The statutes of the Lord are trustworthy,
  making wise the simple. . . .
By them is your servant warned;
  in keeping them there is great reward.
                    PSALM 19:7, 11

God, however, holds each of us personally responsible for our
choices . . . He alone knows whether we have availed ourselves of
the information within our reach regarding some of the conclu-
sions we draw and the actions we . . . take.
                    VERNON GROUNDS
                    ECOLOGY AND LIFE (FOREWORD)

Step by step, one by one, find the actions that suit you best, try
them out, tell your friends, and things will change . . . no matter
what anyone says, you and I do have the power to begin to make
the world a better place.
                    JEFFREY HOLLENDER
                    HOW TO MAKE THE WORLD A
                    BETTER PLACE

❏ Slow down your stream of junk mail

At our house procrastination always wins the day with one
task: going through the mail. If that's true at your house too,
you can easily get rid of about three-fourths of your problem.
And you can cut the paper and energy waste that goes into
creating and delivering almost 2 million tons of junk mail
every year.

Write to the following address, asking them to remove you and everyone in your household from their mailing lists:

● Mail Preference Service
  c/o Direct Mail Association
  11 West Forty-second Street
  P.O. Box 3861
  New York, NY 10163-3861

Be sure to list the appropriate names in all the ways they appear on your various mailings. Writing this letter should eventually eliminate most of the second- and third-class mailings you receive. You may want to contact individually other businesses that continue to mail to you, having obtained your address from other sources. When you do receive junk mail, remember to recycle it along with your other waste paper.

☐ Explore your community to find out about services such as recycling, waste disposal, clean-up programs, and water and energy conservation

If you intend to develop new earth-keeping habits, you will probably need to know about community resources that help you reduce, reuse, and recycle. Your local water and utility companies can no doubt provide you with some resources (energy audits and water conservation kits, for example). Look for additional resources in your local yellow pages under these and similar references: Environment, Ecology, Recycling, Conservation, Car Pool, and Lawn and Garden.

Always keep your eyes and ears open to what other citizens are up to in terms of the environment. As you begin new earth-keeping habits, people are apt to ask about what you're doing, and you'll meet new people who know more than you do. You can learn from this local network.

❏ Refuse to purchase products from manufacturers whose practices endanger the environment or harm wildlife

How do you know which products are made with the good of the earth and its creatures in mind? There are several ways to stay informed. After reading this book, you will have more information at hand that will enable you to better trust your own judgment. You can also keep up with current issues: Read the newspaper, watch TV news, or read news magazines to understand issues such as tropical-forest beef and cruelty-free cosmetics. You might go out of your way to purchase consumer guides to help you shop wisely. See page 142 for information on 3 helpful shopping guides.

❏ Write to manufacturers

If you are concerned about a product, its production, or its packaging, write and express your view to the manufacturer. After all, as the consumer you are the one the manufacturer wants to please.

Product packaging often includes toll-free phone numbers. If you don't have time for a letter, at least place a telephone call. When I've inquired about products or practices, some companies have simply registered my complaint. One company clarified a product's ingredients and sent me a complimentary sample. An airline I frequently travel gave me the good news that they've started a recycling program for their aluminum cans. Responses can surprise you.

❏ Avoid eating processed beef and beef served in fast-food restaurants

Only about 2% of the beef pressed into hamburgers in U.S. fast-food restaurants comes from tropical forests, but even that amount has a devastating effect on that endangered habitat. (Many tropical forest ranchers sell their beef to restaurants in other countries where consumers aren't yet concerned about tropical forest destruction.)

It's almost impossible for a consumer to know which restaurants import beef from tropical forest areas. Consequently, the safest consumer approach is to avoid eating all fast-food beef.

Because beef grown in tropical forest areas tends to be lower quality than beef grown in Australia or the U.S., it is often processed (to camouflage its tough, stringy consistency) and used in products like baby foods, canned and frozen beef products, hot dogs, beef luncheon meats, and soups. Right now, it's safest to avoid these products also. Eventually labeling laws may help consumers identify the geographical source of the beef.

❏ Support local and federal mass-transit funding

Right now, only 1¢ of the 9.1¢-per-gallon federal gasoline tax goes toward public transportation, and 8¢ goes toward building and repairing highways and bridges (*Consumer Reports*, Jan. 1990). Yet most experts agree that an increased reliance on mass, rather than private, transit is essential to stopping the devastating environmental effects of automobiles.

Look for opportunities to support local and federal initiatives and programs for mass transit, bicycle paths, and other alternative methods of transportation.

❏ Vote knowledgeably on environmental issues

Unfortunately, there's no easy way to do this. The only way to vote knowledgeably is to be knowledgeable. That means you're going to have to read about environmental issues and stay informed through newspapers, TV, and magazines. You might consider subscribing to, or checking out from the library, magazines such as *World Watch, Garbage, Project EarthSave, Buzzworm, Audubon Magazine, National Wildlife,* and *International Wildlife.* For a Christian perspective on these issues, look into these periodicals: *Advocate, The Other Side, Action, Christianity Today, Moody Monthly,* and *Sojourners.* (See addresses on page 120.)

An annual update of what's going on in the environment is published in a book called *State of the World,* prepared by Worldwatch Institute. (Check your local library.)

With every passing month and year, you'll find it easier to stay informed about environmental issues. Why? Because they're critical, and they'll be in the news constantly. If enough of us begin adopting earth-keeping behaviors, perhaps there'll be some good news mixed in with the inevitable bad.

❏ Write to elected officials

If you're informed about environmental issues, you'll likely have some opinions. Let your city, state, and federal representatives know what you think. If enough politicians hear concerns voiced by enough constituents, they may speed up the slow-turning wheels of change. Here are some addresses to facilitate your letter writing:

- President of the United States
  Washington, DC 20500

- U.S. Senate
  Washington, DC 20510

- U.S. House of Representatives
  Washington, DC 20515

Check your public library for names and addresses of all your federal, state, and local elected officials.

❏ Support organizations involved in conservation

There are many environmental groups to choose from, each with its unique style, focus, and approach. If you find one or more that you feel comfortable supporting, your dollars will be well spent by experts who know what they want to accomplish and have a plan for making it happen. See page 144 for a partial list of these organizations. Several of the books included in "Earth-Keeping Sources" have more complete listings.

❏ Work in your community to protect the environment

There's a popular "pro-environment" slogan: "Think globally, act locally." Sound advice. Find out how you can help with recycling, beach cleanup, species and habitat protection, hazardous-waste disposal, and other environmental activities in your immediate area.

Approach this habit as you would some of the others: Start small. Increase support as you can. You don't have to volunteer every week; you could start by volunteering once a year or once a month. Or you don't have to volunteer at all. You might provide monetary support by paying dues to a local organization or donating to a one-time event. Whatever support you can give shows your willingness to be a good steward of the earth.

❏ Comment and ask questions when you encounter wasteful or environmentally harmful practices

With your new awareness and as you establish new behaviors, you're going to notice more things that are out of kilter with God's good creation. You'll be frustrated when others abuse the environment. It's appropriate to speak up, but it's important to do so tactfully and sensitively. Not everyone knows what you know; not everyone has had the opportunity to become committed to the habits you've acquired.

Develop some sensitive approaches, learn how to give suggestions, and figure out how to ask the right questions. Remember to be positive and sensitive, so you can present earth-keeping habits as reasonable, responsible, and desirable behaviors.

❏ Model a good-steward lifestyle

Most of the earth-friendly changes you make will be clearly evident to those around you. People will notice your new habits and ask about them.

Your new lifestyle can be contagious. In fact, I hope a full-scale epidemic of earth-keeping behaviors will break out among your family, friends, and acquaintances.

❏ Share what you know with your family, friends, and co-workers

There are some simple and effective things you can do to take a more active role in educating others of your new concerns. First, remove the pages from the back of this book and post them where you and members of your family will see them. Each member of your family might check off the lists at his or her own pace with a different-colored pen. These visible reminders will help your entire family learn new habits and hold members accountable to one another.

At work, you might post environmental tidbits, articles, and ideas on bulletin boards or offer them to the editor of your company's newsletter. Share this book and other educational resources with your friends.

As you reshape your attitude and behaviors, others will see the stewardship in your lifestyle. It's inevitable. When you respond to their questions with confidence and commitment, they'll listen. They'll learn. They might even make earth keeping a habit.

Earth Keeping with Your Influence

☐ Slow down your stream of junk mail.

☐ Explore your community to find out about services such as recycling, waste disposal, clean-up programs, and water and energy conservation.

☐ Refuse to purchase products from manufacturers whose practices endanger the environment or harm wildlife.

☐ Write to manufacturers.

☐ Avoid eating processed beef and beef served in fast-food restaurants.

☐ Support local and federal mass transit funding.

☐ Vote knowledgeably on environmental issues.

☐ Write to elected officials.

☐ Support organizations involved in conservation.

☐ Work in your community to protect the environment.

☐ Comment and/or ask questions when you encounter wasteful or environmentally harmful practices.

☐ Model a good-steward lifestyle.

☐ Share what you know with your family, friends, and co-workers.

You'll find a removable copy of this checklist on page 143.

12
E A R T H K E E P I N G

and the
Christian Lifestyle

From everyone who has been given much, much will be demanded; and from the one who has been entrusted with much, much more will be asked.

LUKE 12:48

If you're reading this book, chances are you're a Christian who is concerned about the environment. But you may have some questions about your personal role in ecology. Does the Bible actually tell us that we should be good stewards of the earth? And why should we work to preserve our environment when the Bible tells us the earth will someday be destroyed by fire?

If you're like me, you probably have an instinctive feeling— even a conviction—that stewardship of the earth is biblical. But let's look at the Scriptures to see what they say. I owe special thanks to Steve Walker—pastor, theologian, and friend—for collaborating with me on this chapter.

❏ Are there environmental commandments?

Perhaps you have already explored the Bible for specific ecological commandments that apply to our world today. I've done some of my own exploring, and such mandates are hard to find.

Calvin DeWitt, director of AuSable Institute (a Christian environmental stewardship institute) says the Bible is "a kind of survival manual for living rightly on Earth" ("Can We Help Save God's Earth?" *ESA Advocate*, April 1990). That is definitely true, but it's nevertheless impossible to put your finger on a thus-says-the-Lord verse: "You shall not litter the ground or pollute my streams; you shall recycle your waste." You can find verses that give guidelines for the use of land and the treatment of creatures (see, for example, Ex. 23:10–12; Deut. 22:6–7) but no references to toxic waste or recycling.

Why? Because the Scriptures were written with sensitivity to a specific time and culture, an agrarian, pre-industrialized society. The world population was a fraction of the more than 5 billion people on earth today. Humans had not yet settled in all parts of the world, packed their landfills to overflowing, polluted their waterways, or chopped down almost all the valued tropical forests.

In light of this, is the Bible relevant to today's overwhelming environmental problems? Definitely. But instead of looking for specific ecological directives, we need to find broader, basic principles we can apply to today's dilemmas.

If you've read the previous chapters, you know dozens of things that are wrong with our environment. But all those facts and statistics are symptoms of underlying ecological problems. What's at the root of these problems? We are. People. You and I. The way we live has environmental consequences. Cleaning up our lives can help clean up the environment. Let's take a look at some of the things we're doing wrong and then see how the Bible would have us change our ways.

❏ We have forgotten to whom the earth belongs

When using resources, how often do you think of them as being creations of the Creator? The earth and everything in it belongs to God; it's just on loan to us. The earth, created by God, existed before any of us did. In fact, in Genesis 1 God himself declared his creation "good" 6 times before adding human life to it. And the earth will be here long after we leave it. Colossians 1:15–16 shows why God created the earth in the first place.

> He is the image of the invisible God, the firstborn over all creation. For by him all things were created: things in heaven and on earth, visible and invisible, whether thrones or powers or rulers or authorities; all things were created by him and for him.

The earth was created for God's pleasure; he takes delight in it. Because God has put us temporarily in charge of his creation, we should handle it with care. In Genesis 1:26, we read that God included people in his perfect creation. He had a specific job in mind for Adam and his descendents: he delegated the care of his creation to us.

As we read on in Genesis, we learn a little more about God's idea of our job description, as delivered to Adam. God put Adam in the Garden of Eden to "work it and take care of it" (Genesis 2:15). Adam was free to use the resources there ("work it"), but he was to use them wisely ("take care of"). "Take care of" (from the Hebrew *shamar*) is variously translated as "guard," "watch," "oversee," "invest care in," "be vigilant for the sake of others," "cultivate," "protect," and "preserve." Those phrases, from words delivered to Adam, leave no doubt about our God-given job description as earth keepers.

❏ We have been selfish and greedy

Have you noticed that it takes a conscious effort to think of others first? Our faulty—perhaps the word is *sinful*—human nature is ready with thoughts and actions that promote number 1. How does environmental behavior fit into this? Quite simply. Most of us who live in North America have more, consume more, and waste more than almost anyone living anywhere else around our globe. When we overconsume, waste, and pollute, we squander resources that could be used by others far away—who as a matter of course live on much less. We also ruin things right here for our immediate neighbors. In fact, we jeopardize the future of our very own children.

Philippians 2:3–4 makes it quite clear how we should treat other people with whom we share the planet.

> Do nothing out of selfish ambition or vain conceit, but in humility consider others better than yourselves. Each of you should look not only to your own interests, but also to the interests of others.

Using our resources wisely and unselfishly is one way we can look "also to the interests of others."

❏ We have felt that we're "above" nature

Human life is obviously different from the other forms of life with which we share the earth. God did create us in his image, and he has offered us eternal life. God has set us apart, that's clear. But it's also clear that God treasures his other creations. Christian environmentalist Calvin DeWitt has pointed out, for example, that "human expansion may not be at the expense of the rest of creation" ("Can We Help Save God's Earth?" *ESA Advocate*, April 1990). When God said in Genesis 1 that the water should "teem with living creatures" (v. 20) and that birds should "increase on the earth" (v. 22), he meant it. Our role as caretakers requires that we take care concerning the earth's ecological balance. Our job is to ensure that the waters are clean and safe for living creatures that "fill the water in the seas" (v. 22) and that habitat destruction doesn't keep birds from flying "above the earth across the expanse of the sky" (v. 20). As caretakers of the earth, we should not exploit nature but enable it to fulfill its own role in glorifying God.

❏ We have failed to see God in his handiwork

It's no accident that the Scriptures are full of nature illustrations. The psalms are full of beautiful word pictures painted in nature's colors. And Jesus himself used nature to help us understand God's love for us. Scripture shows us something we tend to forget: By better understanding God's handiwork, we can better understand him. In fact, Romans 1:20 says that nature itself bears eloquent testimony to its Creator.

> For since the creation of the world God's invisible qualities—his eternal power and divine nature—have been clearly seen, being understood from what has been made, so that men are without excuse.

Pastor Steve Walker puts it like this: "When we destroy the environment and erect our own, we scratch and smudge the window to understanding about him. We block or at least obscure what he has created as a witness to his creative genius." Conversely, if we do our best to care for and appreciate the environment, we enhance our understanding of the One who made our world and has chosen to make eternal life available to us.

❏ We didn't know how to be good stewards of the earth

Maybe we'd do a better job of caring and sharing if we just knew what to do and where to begin. Right? Right. That's why you're reading this. Now you have some ideas about how to care for creation. As you check off new earth-keeping habits, know that your behaviors are making a difference. You are becoming a better steward of God's good earth.

❏ But earth keepers aren't all Christians

At this point in history, it's safe to say that many—probably most—of earth's conscientious keepers are not Christians. Rather, they're people with various, or no religious beliefs who are concerned about the earth because we're making it uninhabitable. They know that very soon—perhaps by the next generation—the earth may be unfit for other species, for ourselves, and for our children.

How do we react to these environmental pioneers? I feel it's time for Christians to wake up and follow their lead. Our motivation may be different from theirs, but we can learn from what they know about the environment.

❏ All Christians should be earth keepers

If you believe that the earth and everything in it was created by God, it's impossible to wriggle out of your earth-keeping responsibilities. We don't need to worry about the prophetic destruction of the earth; that's God's business. Our business is to ensure that during our short stay on earth we don't abuse what came from God's own mind and hands.

Besides, there's a bonus for earth keepers who are Christians: From helping the earth we get not only physical and emotional satisfaction but the *spiritual* satisfaction that comes as we obey our Creator—motivated by our love for God, our concern for others, and our desire to manage well what God has entrusted to us.

As you begin to be a better earth keeper, read and reread Psalm 104. This "ecology" psalm shows how God has woven the strands of his creation together; it tells us that all life depends on him and voices our hope that someday he will make the earth clean and new again.

May the glory of the Lord endure forever;
may the Lord rejoice in his works.
                              PSALM 104:31

In that day I will make a covenant for them
with the beasts of the field and the birds of the air
and the creatures that move along the ground. . . .
so that all may lie down in safety.

HOSEA 2:18

GLOSSARY

The Perils of Planet Earth

Are phosphates really so bad if they can make algae bloom? What's so great about the ozone layer? We've never had to save energy or water before, why do we have to now?

There are more questions than answers about the perils facing our planet. But one thing is clear: We need to understand as much as we can now—and take quick action on what we know.

If you're confused about some of the terms and issues in this book or in newspapers you read, perhaps this glossary will help you. For further reading check also "Earth-Keeping Sources."

Acid rain When released into the air, sulfur and nitrogen oxides—from vehicles and oil-, coal-, and gas-burning power plants—undergo a chemical change. These harmful chemicals then fall back to earth in the form of sulfuric acid and nitric acid mixed with rain, snow, or fog. This "acid rain" pollutes streams, rivers, and forests, potentially destroying plants and animals. The chemical action of acid rain is so strong that it can corrode car finishes and buildings; acid rain has already damaged landmarks such as the Taj Mahal and ancient Mayan temples. Airborne poisons can build up in people's lungs, causing respiratory ailments.

What you can do: Use less energy. Recycle everything you can. Drive less.

Biodegradable Biodegradable materials can decay. They can be broken down by the action of micro-organisms such as bacteria. Organic wastes, including paper and food, can be broken down. That is, they're biodegradable. Inorganic wastes, including plastic containers and polystyrene foam (Styrofoam) cups, are not biodegradable. That is, they will take up space in our landfills forever.

What you can do: Whenever possible purchase, use, and recycle biodegradable products. Recycle any products you buy that are not biodegradable.

Carbon dioxide (CO_2) Carbon dioxide gas exists naturally in our atmosphere. But every year we artificially add an additional 5.5 billion tons of carbon dioxide into the air surrounding our globe. Carbon dioxide is responsible for about 50% of the greenhouse effect or "global warming." Each year each person living in the U.S. contributes about 6 tons of carbon dioxide to the air by using energy from fossil fuels (coal, oil, natural gas).

What you can do: Use less energy. Support tropical forest conservation. Drive less.

Chlorofluorocarbons (CFCs) These industrial chemicals are used in refrigerants, solvents, plastics, foam insulation, and some aerosol sprays. They are responsible for 15% to 20% of the greenhouse effect. When released, CFCs slowly rise to the top layer of the atmosphere. There, when hit by the sun's ultraviolet rays, they break apart, releasing particles of chlorine. Chlorine atoms destroy ozone, a gaseous component of our upper atmosphere. CFCs can last more than 100 years and have already destroyed as much as 5% of our ozone layer.

What you can do: Keep home air conditioners, car air conditioners, and refrigerators in good repair; make sure service technicians capture and recycle CFCs and HCFCs during re-pair/recharging/disposal. Watch for future alternatives to CFCs as coolants in car air conditioners. Avoid purchasing or using products that contain ozone-damaging chemicals.

Dioxins Dioxins are chemicals released during the process of bleaching paper pulp. Their main ingredient is chlorine. When dioxins pollute lakes, rivers, and oceans, they cause deformities and reduced reproduction in marine animals. Chlorinated chemicals can also become concentrated in the bodies of marine animals like fish and crustaceans. When animals—including humans—eat contami-nated fish, they ingest highly concentrated amounts of these harmful chemicals.

Minute amounts of dioxins also stay in paper products, including coffee filters and toilet paper. Even minute amounts of dioxins may suppress immune systems and cause cancer and other diseases.

What you can do: Avoid using bleached paper products.

Endangered According to the World Wildlife Fund, a species is endangered when it "has so few members left that it is in danger of dying out." Scientists estimate that more than 25,000 plant species are endangered—one-tenth of the known species, though not all species of plants or animals are known. In fact, only 1.7 million of earth's 5 to 30 million different species have been identified. Because wild habitats are disappearing so rapidly, species are likely becoming extinct before we can even identify them or classify them as endangered.

What you can do: Support wildlife conservation organizations. Refuse to buy products from imperiled habitats such as tropical forests and wetlands. Don't take exotic plants or animals out of their native habitats. Refuse to buy clothing or accessories (shoes, jewelry, belts) made from reptile skins or other wildlife products.

Extinct When the last of a species dies—be it plant or animal—the species is said to be extinct: gone forever. Some scientists estimate that currently one species on earth becomes extinct every hour. Others estimate that 100 species become extinct every day. Still others say that, by the year 2000, a full 15% of the species now on earth will be extinct.

Most extinctions occur in tropical forests, earth's fastest-disappearing habitat. In all habitats the main cause of extinction is habitat destruction, followed by overhunting. Species have become extinct before in the history of the earth, but never at the current fast and relentless pace.

What you can do: Support wildlife conservation organizations. Refuse to buy products from imperiled habitats, such as tropical forests and wetlands. At home and when you travel, refuse to buy products made from exotic woods, plants, and animals.

Fossil fuel Fossil fuels, such as coal, oil, and natural gas, come from plants and animals that were alive thousands of years ago. When fossil fuels are burned in cars, furnaces, or power plants, carbon dioxide is released into the air and contributes to the greenhouse effect. Americans use more fossil fuel per capita than citizens in any other country. Even though we account for only about 5% of the world's population, we consume more than 30% of the world's resources, including fossil fuel.

What you can do: Use less energy generated by coal, oil, and natural gas.

Global warming Global warming is the result of gases, including carbon dioxide, methane, sulfur dioxide, and nitrous oxide, that we put into the atmosphere. Such pollutants trap heat near the surface of the earth, causing the earth's temperature to rise. This global warming is predicted to increase over the next 50 years, raising global temperatures by as much as 9 Fahrenheit degrees. This may not sound like much, but the effects of that amount of global warming would be devastating: Rising seas would cover low-lying countries and coastal areas; deserts would spread into areas that are now major agricultural regions; water shortages would be world-wide; and raging storms would devastate land areas.

What you can do: Drive less. Avoid products that contain or use CFCs. Use less fossil-fuel energy.

Greenhouse effect Natural gases—including hydrogen, carbon dioxide, and oxygen—wrap around the earth in a thick atmospheric blanket. Like glass in a greenhouse, these gases let sunlight in and keep heat from escaping. When this greenhouse effect functions normally, it keeps our planet warm. But pollution puts dangerous gases—like carbon dioxide, chlorofluorocarbons, ground-level ozone, methane, and nitrous oxide—into our lower atmosphere. These gases trap heat close to the earth's surface and raise our planet's temperature. The term *global warming* is often used synonymously with *greenhouse effect.*

What you can do: Drive less. Avoid products that contain or use CFCs. Use less fossil-fuel energy.

Groundwater Groundwater is simply water that's under the ground. It seeps through cracks and spaces in underground rocks and layers of sediment and stretches in vast subterranean reservoirs called aquifers. Unless contaminated by chemicals, most groundwater has percolated for years through earth's rocky filtering system and is naturally pure. Only 1% of earth's water is drinkable (not salty or frozen), and more than 90% of that drinkable water is groundwater. Over half the U.S. population uses groundwater for drinking. Some groundwater reservoirs are in deep, inaccessible pockets that can never be replenished. The remaining aquifers are not quickly replenished from snow or rain, unlike above-ground lakes and streams. And groundwater contamination is widespread across the United States. Our wasteful and careless practices in water use could result in some aquifers drying up within 40 to 50 years, sinking land areas in some locations, and severe water shortages in many states.

What you can do: Dispose of hazardous materials properly, not by pouring chemicals down the drain or onto the ground. Conserve water.

Halons Halons are chemicals that, along with chlorofluorocarbons (CFCs), damage our ozone layer. Halons release bromine—a red, smelly, corrosive, toxic element.

What you can do: Refuse to buy halon fire extinguishers.

Hazardous waste Hazardous waste is the unused portion of any product that contains toxic chemicals. Every year, people in the United States discard hundreds of tons of hazardous substances, including household cleaners, automotive fluids, paints, solvents, and pesticides. (See page 136 for a more complete list.)

What you can do: Create less hazardous waste by using less-toxic products. Dispose of hazardous waste properly.

Leachate This liquid results when water leaches—percolates down through—the ground. Leachate from landfills can contain decomposed waste, bacteria, and chemicals. It can flow into our waterways or seep into groundwater, causing contamination.

What you can do: Dispose of hazardous waste at special collection centers, not with trash that goes to your landfill. Use less-toxic products.

Methane Methane makes up almost 20% of the gases responsible for global warming. It is produced by cattle, rice fields, and landfills in which organic waste is breaking down.

What you can do: Eat less beef. Reduce waste.

Nitrous oxide This gas makes up about 10% of the gases responsible for global warming. It is produced by the action of microbes (microscopic organisms such as bacteria) in the soil, by the decomposition of chemical fertilizers, and by burning wood and fossil fuels.

What you can do: Reduce energy use. Avoid burning wood or charcoal. Avoid using chemical fertilizers.

Nonrenewable resources Nonrenewable resources are elements and compounds in our world that, once they're used up, cannot be replaced. Petroleum, and bauxite are examples of nonrenewable resources.

What you can do: Avoid using products made from nonrenewable resources whenever possible. If you must use products made from nonrenewable resources, recycle them if you can (e.g., aluminum cans). Especially avoid products, including plastics, that use petroleum. Drive less and drive conservatively.

Ozone layer In our planet's upper atmosphere, a gas called ozone forms a thin, protective layer that keeps harmful ultraviolet radiation from the sun from penetrating to earth. When we use products that contain chlorofluorocarbons (CFCs), halons, carbon tetrachloride, methyl chloroform, and hydrochlorofluorocarbons (HCFCs), we endanger this vital protective shield wrapped around our planet. We already have 2 and possibly 3 holes in our ozone layer. Scientists predict that by the year 2050 the ozone layer will be diminished by 10%. If that happens, people will experience dramatically increased occurrences of skin cancer; people and animals will suffer severe damage to their immune systems with inevitable infections and diseases; and plants will succumb to radiation, with resulting losses of food crops.

What you can do: Keep home air conditioners, car air conditioners, and refrigerators in good repair; make sure service technicians capture and recycle CFCs and HCFCs during repair/recharging/disposal. Watch for future alternatives to CFCs as coolants in car air conditioners. Avoid purchasing or using products that contain ozone-damaging chemicals.

Ozone smog Ozone, so essential in the earth's upper atmosphere, is also formed at ground level, where it can be deadly. Ozone is the primary component of smog and comes from motor vehicles, power plants, and oil refineries.

What you can do: Reduce car use. Keep your car well maintained. Use less energy.

Phosphates Phosphates are chemical compounds that contain phosphorus. They occur in many laundry detergents. When phosphates get into streams and lakes, they fertilize algae, causing it to grow out of control. When this "algae bloom" subsides, the algae die and the decay process uses up the oxygen needed by other water plants and marine life. In severe cases, a stream's entire ecosystem can die.

What you can do: Use laundry soap or phosphate-free detergents.

Photodegradable Some plastics are manufactured so they break down when exposed to the sun's ultraviolet rays. But these photodegradable plastics don't really decompose; they just break into small pieces. Additionally, ultraviolet rays never reach plastics that are buried in dark landfills.

What you can do: Avoid using photodegradable plastic products.

Polystyrene foam (Styrofoam) This type of plastic has several severe problems: It never decomposes; it is made from petroleum, a nonrenewable resource; its manufacture can produce chlorofluorocarbons and other smog-producing by-products; it kills marine animals that ingest it; and it takes up more than its share of space in landfills because of its high air content. Polystyrene foam can be recycled, but is not now recycled on a large scale. When recycled, it can be incorporated into the production of "plastic lumber," a new product that could help save forests.

What you can do: Refuse to buy products made from or packaged in polystyrene foam.

Precycling Precycling is a way to reduce waste before it has a chance to become waste. People who choose not to buy something for environmental reasons are practicing precycling. A shopper might choose to precycle (choose not to buy a product) because a product has excessive packaging, is made from unrecyclable materials, or might harm the environment in any number of other ways.

What you can do: Apply what you know about environment-friendly products when you shop. Buy products that do not harm the environment.

Recycling Recycling occurs when used or waste products are incorporated into the manufacture of the same or another product. For instance, when paper is recycled, it can be made into "new" paper or paper products. Recycling uses fewer resources, less energy, and is less polluting than creating products from new materials.

What you can do: Recycle paper, newspaper, aluminum, glass, cardboard, steel cans, plastics, and any other products your recycling center accepts.

Renewable resources Renewable resources are resources that can be replaced. For instance, wood is renewable because trees can grow to replace used wood.

What you can do: If you have a choice between purchasing a product made from renewable versus nonrenewable resources, choose the one made from renewable resources. Recycle.

Sanitary landfill Sanitary landfills are designated areas where refuse can be deposited in a controlled, environmentally safe way. Landfills are specially prepared to control water drainage and to confine refuse to the smallest possible volume. When landfills are full, they can be used for parks or other recreational uses. Unfortunately, our landfills are filling up too fast. Some predict that more than half of the 9,300 landfills in the U.S. will be full and forced to close within 10 years. Our tremendous waste stream comes in part from 4 to 6 pounds of trash produced by every American every day. In New York City, that adds up to 25,000 tons of waste daily.

What you can do: Reduce your waste by precycling, reusing, recycling, and composting.

Sulfur dioxide (SO$_2$) This gas is released when coal and some types of oil are burned. Sulfur dioxide changes in the atmosphere to sulfuric acid, then falls back to earth mixed with rain, snow, and fog. This resulting "acid rain" damages buildings and forests and has acidified lakes, streams, rivers, and even our soil.

What you can do: Reduce your car use. Reduce your energy use.

Tropical forests Lush tropical forests cover only about 7% of our planet, yet they house 50% to 80% of the earth's species. Incredibly, these rich tropical forest habitats are being logged and burned down at the rate of 100 acres a minute, around the clock. Not only are we losing important crop and medicinal species daily, but we are losing one of our best defenses against global warming: trees that consume carbon dioxide, a poisonous gas spewed constantly into the atmosphere by our cars and power plants. Some estimates predict that by the end of this century, 80% of these irreplaceable habitats will be gone forever.

What you can do: Avoid purchasing any product that comes from tropical forest agriculture or logging, including tropical-forest-grown beef and tropical woods. (See page 128 for a list of tropical woods to avoid.) Support tropical forest conservation organizations. Plant trees.

SOURCES

The factual information in *Earth Keeping* comes from hundreds of books, periodicals, pamphlets, and fact sheets, including the titles listed in this chapter. All the sources listed here are especially helpful references for further reading. For a more complete list of reading resources, purchase or check out from the library a copy of the book, *The Green Consumer*.

Books

Badke, William B. *Project Earth: Preserving the World God Created.* Portland, Ore.: Multnomah Press, 1991.

The Bennett Information Group. *The Green Pages: Your Everyday Shopping Guide to Environmentally Safe Products.* New York: Random House, 1990.

Bhagat, Shantilal P. *Creation in Crisis: Responding to God's Covenant.* Elgin, Ill.: Brethren Press, 1990.

Brown, Lester R., et al. *State of the World.* New York: W. W. Norton, 1990.

Dadd, Debra Lynn. *The Nontoxic Home.* Los Angeles: Jeremy P. Tarcher, 1986.

The Earth Works Group. *50 Simple Things You Can Do to Save the Earth.* Berkeley, Calif.: Earth Works Press, 1989.

Elkington, John and Julia Hailes and Joel Makower. *The Green Consumer.* New York: Viking Penguin, 1990.

Elsdon, Ron. *Bent World: A Christian Response to the Environmental Crisis.* Downers Grove, Ill.: InterVarsity Press, 1981.

Gladwin, John. *God's People in God's World: Biblical Motives for Social Involvement.* Downers Grove, Ill.: InterVarsity Press, 1979.

Granberg-Michaelson, Wesley. *Ecology and Life: Accepting Our Environmental Responsibility.* Irving, Tex.: Word, 1988.

Granberg-Michaelson, Wesley. *A Worldly Spirituality: The Call to Redeem Life on Earth.* San Francisco: Harper & Row, 1984.

Hall, Douglas John. *The Steward: A Biblical Symbol Come of Age.* Grand Rapids: Eerdmans, 1990.

Heloise. *Heloise: Hints for a Healthy Planet.* New York: Putnam, 1990.

Hesterman, Vicki, ed. *The Earth Is the Lord's: Handle with Care.* Napoleon, Ohio: Accord Publishing House, 1990.

Hollender, Jeffrey. *How to Make the World a Better Place: A Guide to Doing Good.* New York: William Morrow, 1990.

Hynes, Patricia. *Earth Right, Every Citizen's Guide.* Rocklin, Calif.: Prima Publishing, 1990.

Lamb, Marjorie. *2 Minutes a Day for a Greener Planet.* New York: Harper & Row, 1990.

Lappe, Frances Moore. *Diet for a Small Planet.* New York: Ballantine, 1971, 1975, 1982.

Longacre, Doris Janzen. *Living More with Less.* Scottdale, Pa.: Herald, 1980.

MacEachern, Diane. *Save Our Planet, 750 Everyday Ways You Can Help Clean Up the Earth.* New York: Bantam Doubleday Dell, 1990.

The Presbyterian Eco-Justice Task Force. *Keeping and Healing the Creation.* [Louiseville, Ky.: Presbyterian Church (U.S.A.), 1989.

Rifkin, Jeremy, ed. *The Green Lifestyle Handbook: 1001 Ways You Can Heal the Earth.* New York: Henry Holt, 1990.

Schaeffer, Francis A. *Pollution and the Death of Man.* Wheaton, Ill.: Tyndale House, 1970.

Sider, Ronald J., ed. *Lifestyle in the Eighties: An Evangelical Commitment to Simple Lifestyle.* Louisville, Ky.: Westminster, 1982.

Sombke, Laurence. *The Solution to Pollution, 101 Things You Can Do to Clean Up Your Environment.* New York: MasterMedia Limited, 1990.

Wilkinson, Loren, ed. *Earthkeeping: Christian Stewardship of Natural Resources.* Grand Rapids: Eerdmans, 1980.

Will, Rosalyn and Alice Tepper Marlin, Benjamin Corson, and Jonathan Schorsch. *Shopping for a Better World, a Quick and Easy Guide to Socially Responsible Supermarket Shopping.* New York: Council on Economic Priorities, 1989.

Periodicals

ACTION (National Association of Evangelicals, 450 Gundersen Drive, Carol Stream, IL 60188).

Advocate (Evangelicals for Social Action, 10 Lancaster Avenue, Philadelphia, PA 19151).

Buzzworm: The Environmental Journal (1818 Sixteenth Street, Boulder, CO 80302).

Christianity and Crisis: A Christian Journal of Opinion (Christianity and Crisis, Inc., 537 West 121 Street, New York, NY 10027).

Consumer Reports (Consumers Union of U.S. Inc., 256 Washington Street, Mount Vernon, NY 10553).

Garbage: The Practical Journal for the Environment (435 Ninth Street, Brooklyn, NY 11215).

Home Energy (2124 Kittredge Street, Suite 95, Berkeley, CA 94704).

The Other Side (300 West Apsley Street, Philadelphia, PA 19144).

Sojourners (P.O. Box 29272, Washington, DC 20017).

World Watch (Worldwatch Institute, 1776 Massachusetts Avenue NW, Washington, DC 20036).

Pamphlets, Fact Sheets, Brochures

Energy: 101 Practical Tips for Home and Work. (The Windstar Foundation, Snowmass, CO 81654).

FRAGILE: Handle with Care . . . an Earth Keeping Handbook (Agricultural Concerns Committee, Mennonite Central Committee Ontario, 50 Kent Avenue, Kitchener, ON N2G 3R1, Canada).

Heating with Wood (U.S. Department of Energy, Washington, DC 20585).

"Home Safe Home" fact sheets (Environmental Health Coalition, 1844 Third Avenue, San Diego, CA 92101).

101 Ways to Help Heal the Earth (The Greenhouse Crisis Foundation, 1130 Seventeenth Street NW, Washington, DC 20036).

Rainforest Action Guide (Rainforest Action Network, 301 Broadway, Suite A, Department P, San Francisco, CA 94133-9846).

Saving the Ozone Layer (Natural Resources Defense Council, 40 West Twentieth Street, New York, NY 10011).

Tips for Energy Savers (U.S. Department of Energy, Washington, DC 20585).

Winter Survival, A Consumer's Guide to Winter Preparedness (U.S. Department of Energy, Washington, DC 20585).

EARTH KEEPING
Habits

Lists to Post

The lists on the following pages are included so you can remove them from the book and post them where you'll see them. Keeping these lists visible as you move through your day can help you and your family permanently incorporate new earth-keeping behaviors.

On the back of the lists you'll find helpful resources mentioned in preceding chapters.

Earth Keeping in Your Kitchen

- ❏ Rinse dishes in a pan, not under running water.
- ❏ Use energy-efficient cycles on your dishwasher. Wash full loads. Air dry dishes.
- ❏ Use a spatula—not running water—to remove food from dishes.
- ❏ Keep a bottle of drinking water in the refrigerator.
- ❏ Set your refrigerator thermostat at 38 to 42 degrees. Keep it clean and in good repair. Open it as little as possible.
- ❏ Use the stove, microwave, toaster oven, or pressure cooker instead of a conventional oven.
- ❏ Bake several items at once; keep your oven closed.
- ❏ Eat—and serve—less meat.
- ❏ Use cloth—not paper—napkins, towels, and rags.
- ❏ Store food in reusable containers.
- ❏ Use cold water instead of hot whenever possible.
- ❏ Fit pots to burners and amounts of food; use lids.
- ❏ Use a permanent coffee filter, not disposables.
- ❏ Line trash cans with newspapers or paper bags instead of plastic.
- ❏ Cut the rings on plastic holders of 6-pack cans.
- ❏ Recycle aluminum, glass, cardboard, and plastic.

This list could go on your refrigerator, kitchen cupboard, or above your sink.

Kitchen and Household Supplies:

These companies can supply you with earth-friendly kitchen and household supplies—natural cleaners, cloth or string shopping bags, recycled paper products, and more.

Ashdun Industries
400 Sylvan Avenue
Englewood Cliffs, NJ 07632
800-327-4386

Ecco Bella
6 Provost Square, Suite 602
Caldwell, NJ 07006
800-283-4747

Co-Op America
2100 M Street NW, Suite 403
Washington, DC 20063
800-424-2667

The Nature of Things
3956 Long Place
Carlsbad, CA 92008
800-726-4480

Earth Care Paper Company
P.O Box 14140
Madison, WI 53714-0140
608-277-2900

Seventh Generation
Colchester, VT 05446-1672
800-456-1177

Recycling Resources If you have difficulty finding recycling resources in your area, check these sources:

Environmental Defense Fund
257 Park Avenue South
New York, NY 10010
Environmental Defense Fund
hotline: 800-CALL-EDF

National Recycling Coalition
1101 Thirtieth Street NW
Suite 305
Washington, DC 20007
202-625-6406

U. S. Environmental Protection Agency
401 M Street SW
Washington, DC 20460
EPA waste hotline: 800-424-9346

Earth Keeping in Your Living Room

❏ Recycle your newspapers.

❏ Share magazine and newspaper subscriptions.

❏ Close the fireplace damper when you're not using your fireplace.

❏ Use your fireplace rarely; consider installing a wood-burning stove or fireplace insert.

❏ Turn heat or air conditioning to the temperature you want, not higher or lower.

❏ Clean and replace air conditioner and furnace filters regularly.

❏ Keep home air conditioning equipment in good repair; make sure vapors are recovered during servicing.

❏ At night and when you leave home for several hours: In winter lower your furnace thermostat setting. In summer raise your air conditioner setting.

❏ In winter open drapes to let in sunshine. In summer close them against the sunshine.

❏ Install ceiling fans to circulate air.

❏ Dress warmer in winter and cooler in summer to minimize the use of heaters and air conditioners.

❏ Use compact fluorescent light bulbs wherever you can; install dimmer switches on other fixtures.

❏ Avoid buying furniture and accessories made from tropical woods.

This list could go near your TV, thermostat, or a main light switch.

Resources for Using Energy Efficiently:

Hassol, Susan, and Beth Richman. *Energy: 101 Practical Tips for Home and Work.* Snowmass, Colo.: The Windstar Foundation, 1989. (To obtain a price list, write: The Windstar Foundation, 2317 Snomass Creek Rd., Snowmass, CO 81654 or call 303-927-4777.)

Home Energy Magazine's 1991 Consumer Guide to Home Energy Savings. Berkeley, Calif.: Energy Auditor & Retrofitter.

List of Tropical Woods to Avoid: The following list is compiled by the Rainforest Action Network. For more information, look for *The Wood Users Guide* by Pamela Wellner and Eugene Dickey (San Francisco: Rainforest Action Network, 1991).

Apitong	*Malaysia, Thailand, Philippines*
Balsa	*Central and South America*
Banak	*Central and South America*
Bocote	*Central and South America*
Bubinga	*West Africa*
Cocobolo	*Central America*
Cordia	*Central and South America*
Ebony, African	*Africa*
Ebony, Macassar	*East Indies*
Goncalo alves	*Brazil, northern South America*
Greenheart	*Central America*
Iroko	*West Coast of Africa*
Jelutang	*Malaysia, Brunei*
Koa	*Hawaii*
Lauan	*Philippines*
Mahogany, Honduran	*Central and northern South America*
Mahogany, Philippine	*Philippines*
Meranti	*Malaysia*
Padauk, African	*Central and western tropical Africa*
Padauk, Andaman	*Andaman Islands*
Purpleheart	*Central and northern South America*
Ramin	*Indonesia, Malaysia*
Rosewood, Honduran	*Central America*
Satinwood	*India, Sri Lanka*
Teak	*India, Burma, Thailand, Indo-China, Java; also planted in eastern and western Africa and West Indies*
Virola	*Central America and Venezuela*
Wenge	*Zaire*
Zebrawood	*Gaboon, African Cameroon, West Africa*

Earth Keeping in Your Bathroom

❏ Take a short shower or a shallow bath.

❏ Install a low-flow shower head.

❏ Use less shampoo, conditioner, deodorant, and soap.

❏ Turn off the water while you lather your hair and body in the shower, brush your teeth, and shave.

❏ Turn on the water less than full force when rinsing your hands, teeth, or body.

❏ Install faucet aerators.

❏ Use products that are packaged most sensibly, for example, toothpaste in a tube, not a pump; sanitary supplies without individual wrapping.

❏ Use unscented deodorants, shampoos, lotions, and soaps.

❏ Avoid using aerosol sprays.

❏ Use a permanent razor instead of disposables.

❏ Flush the toilet less often.

❏ Keep a bucket in the shower to catch the water you run while you're waiting for it to warm up.

❏ Displace the water in your toilet tank with a jar, bag, or toilet dam.

❏ Clean with natural products.

This list could go on your bathroom mirror or on the back of the bathroom door.

Less-toxic Bathroom Cleaners:

Check this list for some nontoxic bathroom cleaners you can make easily and economically at home:

Glass and/or mirrors: Mix 1/4 cup vinegar with 1 quart water.

Mildew: Scrub with baking soda or borax. If you avoid rinsing, it will inhibit future mold growth.

Toilet: Sprinkle baking soda or borax on a toilet brush; scrub.

Tub and tile: Scrub with baking soda.

Air freshener: Combine vinegar, a few cloves, and some cinnamon in a small glass jar. Heat in microwave 30-60 seconds, then set in bathroom.

Some Sources for Earth-Friendly Cleaning Products: If you prefer to buy ready-made cleaning products, choose from these products: Bon Ami, Breeze, Simple Green, Ivory Snow, Instant Power. Or request catalogs from mail-order companies, including those mentioned on page 126 and:

AFM Enterprises Inc.
1140 Stacy Court
Riverside, CA 92507
714-781-6860

CHIP Distribution
P.O. Box 704
Manhattan Beach, CA 90266
213-545-5928

Scotch Corporation
P.O. Box 4466
617 East Tenth Street
Dallas, TX 75208
214-943-4605

Shaklee
97 Blanchard Road
Cambridge, MA 02138
617-547-7600

Earth Keeping in Your Bedroom and Baby's Room

❏ Use cedar chips rather than mothballs.

❏ Avoid heating and cooling spare bedrooms.

❏ Sell or give away unwanted clothing.

❏ Reuse unwearable panty hose.

❏ Give excess clothes hangers to a friend or a dry cleaner who will use them.

❏ Choose natural fibers for sheets, towels, and clothing.

❏ Refuse to purchase clothing or accessories made from wild animals.

❏ Use 1 large bulb rather than 2 smaller bulbs in a multi-bulb light fixture.

❏ Turn off the light when you leave the room.

❏ Install efficient lighting when you redecorate.

❏ Wear warm pajamas; snuggle under insulated blankets rather than an electric blanket.

❏ Choose a conventional mattress and springs rather than a waterbed that requires a heater.

❏ Use cloth diapers whenever possible.

❏ Use a washcloth and water rather than disposable paper wipes when you change your baby's diaper.

This list could go on your night stand, closet door, or bedroom mirror.

Lighting Resources:

These resources can help you light your home efficiently:

"Should You Change that Light Bulb?" *Consumer Reports*, January 1990, vol. 55, no. 1, pp. 20–24. This helpful article rates light bulbs in several categories, including cost, length of life, and energy efficiency.

"Lighting the Way Towards More Efficient Lighting." *Home Energy*, January–February 1989, vol. 6, no. 1, pages 16–23. This article can help you choose efficient bulbs that fit your lifestyle and your fixtures.

White Electric Co.: The Light Bulb Place (1511 San Pablo Avenue, Berkeley, CA 94702; 800-468-2852). Send a self-addressed, stamped envelope and ask for information on energy-saving light bulbs, including compact fluorescents.

Avoiding Indoor Pollution

The Inside Story: A Guide to Indoor Air Quality (U.S. Environmental Protection Agency, 401 M Street SW, Washington, DC 20460; 202-382-2080). This useful guide discusses indoor air contamination, including "sick building syndrome."

Earth Keeping in Your Laundry Room

❏ Use a phosphate-free detergent.

❏ Use less of all soaps, softeners, and cleaning products.

❏ Set your water heater at 130 degrees.

❏ Insulate your water heater.

❏ Run your washer only when you have a full load.

❏ Reduce your overall amount of laundry.

❏ Wash with cold water whenever possible.

❏ Dry consecutive loads of clothes and sort clothes by weight.

❏ Keep your dryer's lint filter and outside vent clean.

❏ Hang clothes to dry whenever possible.

❏ Use less-toxic household cleaners whenever possible.

❏ Avoid using products with methyl chloroform.

❏ Avoid using bleach.

❏ Avoid using your washer and dryer between 5:00 P.M. and 7:00 P.M.

This list could go above your washer or dryer or near your cleaning supplies.

Less-toxic Household Cleaners

All-purpose cleaner: Mix 1 quart warm water, 1 teaspoon liquid soap, 1 teaspoon borax or T.S.P. Cleaner, and a small amount of lemon juice or vinegar. Use this solution to clean counters, floors, walls, rugs, upholstery.

Whitener: Use 1/2 cup of borax in each load of laundry to whiten and remove spots. Hang laundry in sun. If you must use bleach, choose a nonchlorine, dry bleach.

Degreaser: Use Simple Green or Breeze.

Laundry spot remover: Squirt with diluted Breeze or other biodegradable cleaner.

Fabric softener: Use half-strength liquid softener or nonperfumed fabric softener. Avoid overdrying clothes. Hang clothes to dry when possible.

Floors: Mix 1/2 cup vinegar or 1/4 cup borax or T.S.P. Cleaner with 1 gallon water for vinyl floors. Use Castile soap or Murphy Oil Soap to damp-mop wood floors.

Furniture polish: Mix a few drops of lemon juice with 1 pint mineral oil and apply with a soft cloth.

Oven: Mix 2 or more tablespoons of baking soda, T.S.P. Cleaner, or borax in 1 gallon of water. Scrub with very fine steel wool. Try scrubbing with pumice on baked-on spots.

Rugs: Spot-clean with diluted Breeze, or use all-purpose cleaner above.

Water Heater Tips: You can double the life of your water heater with preventive maintenance. First, check the anode (the rod that's suspended inside your tank from the top) and replace it when necessary. Second, replace the dip tube with one that's curved to direct water around the periphery of the tank to help reduce sediment. You may be able to perform this maintenance by yourself, or you can hire a plumber to do it. For more detailed information, contact: Elemental Enterprises (P.O. Box 928, Monterey, CA 93942; 408-394-7077).

Earth Keeping in Your Garage and Workshop

- ❏ Use latex, not oil-based, paint.
- ❏ Clean paintbrushes and dispose of paint safely.
- ❏ Store and dispose of hazardous materials properly.
- ❏ Avoid buying halon fire extinguishers.
- ❏ Buy workshop supplies (nails, screws, etc.) in bulk, then store them in reusable kitchen containers (yogurt cups, baby food jars, cans with lids).
- ❏ When you clean out your garage, have a garage sale or give away unwanted items.
- ❏ Use castor oil or mineral oil to lubricate squeaky hinges, reluctant locks, stiff doorknobs, and noisy garage doors.
- ❏ Check for leaks in faucets and toilets and repair them as soon as you can.
- ❏ Use a battery recharger and rechargeable batteries.
- ❏ Check yearly for leaks around windows and doors; caulk and weatherstrip as needed.
- ❏ Install storm or other insulating-type windows.
- ❏ Insulate your walls and attic.

This list could go above your workbench or in your garage.

Hazardous Household Materials:

If you're wondering exactly what constitutes hazardous waste, check this partial list of hazardous products you might have around the house. If they're in your home, be sure to keep them out of reach from pets and children. Then be sure to dispose of them at a hazardous-waste site.

aerosols
all-purpose cleaners
ammonia
antifreeze
automobile cleaner
batteries
brake fluid
chlorine bleach
cosmetics
detergents
disinfectants
drain opener
furniture polish
gasoline
glass cleaner
herbicides
insecticides
lighter fluid
mothballs

motor oil
oven cleaner
paint
paint thinner
pesticides
rodent poison
rubber cement
rug and upholstery cleaner
scouring powder
silver polish
snail and slug killers
toilet bowl cleaner
transmission fluid
tub and tile cleaner
turpentine
varnish
water seal
wood finish

Some Sources for Natural Paint and Building Products

AFM Enterprises
1140 Stacy Court
Riverside, CA 93507
714-781-6860

Livos Plant Chemistry
2641 Cerrillos Road
Santa Fe, NM 87501
505-988-9111

Sinan Company Natural Building Materials
P.O. Box 857
Davis, CA 95617-0857
916-753-3104

Earth Keeping in Your Yard

☐ Clean driveways, walks, and patios with a broom.

☐ Avoid using lighter fluid to light coals for outdoor cooking.

☐ Attract wild birds to your yard.

☐ Water deeply in mornings or evenings.

☐ Keep your mower blades sharp and set them high.

☐ Take plastic pots and trays back to your local plant nursery.

☐ Landscape with low-maintenance, drought-tolerant plants.

☐ Plant trees, shrubs, and other leafy plants rather than large lawns.

☐ Use grass clippings for mulch and/or compost.

☐ Build and use a compost pile.

☐ Control pests naturally and use organic fertilizer.

☐ Plant a garden.

☐ Water with soaker hoses or drip irrigation wherever possible.

☐ Plant shade trees near your house.

This list could go near your gardening supplies or lawn mower.

Information on Composting
and Chemical-free Gardening

Some of the mail-order catalogs listed below offer products and (in some cases) information on organic gardening. In addition, local nurseries and gardening centers are beginning to have much more information and more products available on "green" gardening. These excellent resources are also available at libraries and bookstores.

Editors and staff of *Organic Gardening®* magazine. *The Encyclopedia of Organic Gardening: New Revised Edition.* Emmaus, PA: Rodale Press, Inc., 1978.

Editors of Sunset Books and *Sunset* magazine. *Sunset: An Illustrated Guide to Organic Gardening.* Menlo Park, Calif.: Sunset Publishing Corp., 1991.

"The Green Way to a Green Yard." *Consumer Reports,* June 1991, vol. 56, no. 6, pp. 407–22. This article offers information on mulching mowers, chippers and shredders, and organic methods of weed and pest control.

Some Sources for Natural Pesticides and Fertilizers

Gardener's Supply
128 Intervale Road
Burlington, VT 05401
802-863-1700

Growing Naturally
P.O. Box 54
Pineville, PA 18946
215-598-7025

Necessary Trading Company
One Nature's Way
New Castle, VA 24127
800-447-5354

Ringer
9959 Valley View Road
Eden Prairie, MN 55344-3585
800-654-1047

Backyard Wildlife Refuge

Consumer Information Catalog
Pueblo, CO 81009

Invite Wildlife to Your Backyard
National Wildlife Federation
1400 Sixteenth Street NW
Washington, DC 20036-2266

Earth Keeping in Your Car

☐ If your car idles more than a minute, turn it off.

☐ Use a trigger nozzle and bucket when washing your car.

☐ Avoid topping off your gas tank.

☐ Use unleaded gasoline if possible.

☐ Drive smoothly: Speed up and slow down gradually. Avoid tailgating. Don't exceed 55 miles per hour.

☐ Plan your trips carefully: Combine errands. Plan your route. Call ahead.

☐ Carpool whenever possible—to work, church, and social events.

☐ Drive less. Bike, walk, and use public transportation more.

☐ Avoid drive-through lines and rush-hour traffic.

☐ Keep your car's air conditioner in good repair; choose a service station that captures and recycles air conditioner refrigerant.

☐ Properly inflate, balance, and rotate your tires.

☐ Use radial tires, especially steel-belted radials.

☐ Choose service stations that recycle brake fluid, oil, batteries, tires, and air conditioner refrigerant.

☐ Service your car regularly. Keep all filters clean.

☐ When you buy a car, choose a fuel-efficient model.

This list could go on your car's visor or dashboard.

Planting Trees to Combat Carbon Dioxide:

Trees consume carbon dioxide—from 16 to 48 pounds of it per tree per year. So the more trees we plant, the more we help offset our carbon dioxide excess. For local programs check out Arbor Day events and activities and local garden and horticultural clubs. Contact these national organizations if you'd like to help green up our planet:

American Forestry Association
P.O. Box 2000
Washington, DC 20013
202-667-3300
Inquire about their Global Re-Leaf campaign and its goal to plant 100 million trees in America.

National Arbor Day Foundation
100 Arbor Ave.
Nebraska City, NE 68410
This organizaiton provides information on planting and growing trees

Floresta U.S.A., Inc.
1015 Chestnut Avenue, Suite F2
Carlsbad, CA 92008
619-434-6311
This biblically based organization ministers to people's physical and spiritual needs through unique and creative reforestation projects.

Trees for Life
1103 Jefferson
Wichita, KS 67203
316-263-7294
This secular organization distributes seedlings for food and fuel in deforested countries, particularly India.

The Nature Conservancy
1815 North Lynn Street
Arlington, VA 22209
703-841-5300
Inquire about their Tree Program.

Worldwatch Institute
1776 Massachusetts Avenue NW
Washington, DC 20036
202-452-1999
Ask for price list for World Watch Papers, including #83, "Reforesting the Earth."

Earth Keeping at the Grocery Store

❑ Refuse to buy products packaged in polystyrene foam (Styrofoam).

❑ If you don't need a bag, don't take one.

❑ Leave the plastic bag fasteners at the store.

❑ Take your own paper, cloth, or string bags to the store.

❑ Keep extra shopping bags in your car.

❑ Choose products with the least packaging.

❑ Choose products sold in recycled or recyclable packaging.

❑ Buy in bulk whenever possible.

❑ Buy the largest package possible.

❑ Be aware of environment-friendly products of all kinds and buy those brands.

❑ Read labels before you buy.

❑ Avoid buying products that contain chlorofluorocarbons (CFCs).

❑ Buy organic, locally grown foods in season.

❑ Buy unbleached products whenever possible.

*This list could go in your kitchen, car, or with
your shopping list or coupons.*

Some Earth-Friendly Products:

The following list is from *The Green Consumer,* which says these products deserve special merit for their earth-friendly approaches. Watch for these products in your store and look for others that incorporate similar earth-friendly characteristics.

C.A.R.E. products—these "Consumer Action to Restore the Environment" products are made from recycled materials and without using chlorine bleach. Look for paper napkins, towels, toilet paper, tissue, and coffee filters as well as cotton balls and swabs.

Downey Fabric Softener refills—Procter and Gamble offers fabric softener in a 64-ounce, refillable plastic jug. The jug can be reused with refills packaged in carton-like cardboard containers.

Fountain Fresh soda—if this product is offered in your area, you can purchase 2-liter bottles, then take them back to selected stores for refills. A machine washes and refills your bottle, and you take away your refill for 30¢ less than you paid for the first bottle.

Melitta Natural coffee filters—if you can locate this brand, you can purchase unbleached-paper coffee filters and help stop dioxin contamination.

Pillsbury Microwave cake mixes—after you buy the first cake mix, complete with pan, you can buy refills and reuse the pan.

Scotch Corporation concentrates—look for small plastic pouches of household and glass cleaner. You buy the cleaner and a spray bottle and add water at home. This product saves on packaging and energy costs in transporting it, and allows you to reuse your spray bottle.

Wm. T. Thompson Company vitamins—this company changed from plastic to glass containers and uses recycled packaging materials.

Some Helpful Shopping Guides:

Elkington, John and Julia Hailes and Joel Makower. *The Green Consumer.* New York: Penguin, 1990.

The Bennett Information Group. *The Green Pages: Your Everyday Shopping Guide to Environmentally Safe Products.* New York: Random House, 1990.

Will, Rosalyn, Alice Tepper Marlin, Benjamin Corson, and Jonathan Schorsch. *Shopping for a Better World.* New York: Council on Economic Priorities, 1989.

Earth Keeping with Your Influence

☐ Slow down your stream of junk mail.

☐ Explore your community to find out about services such as recycling, waste disposal, clean-up programs, and water and energy conservation.

☐ Refuse to purchase products from manufacturers whose practices endanger the environment or harm wildlife.

☐ Write to manufacturers.

☐ Avoid eating processed beef and beef served in fast-food restaurants.

☐ Support local and federal mass transit funding.

☐ Vote knowledgeably on environmental issues.

☐ Write to elected officials.

☐ Support organizations involved in conservation.

☐ Work in your community to protect the environment.

☐ Comment and/or ask questions when you encounter wasteful or environmentally harmful practices.

☐ Model a good-steward lifestyle.

☐ Share what you know with your family, friends, and co-workers.

This list could go on a bulletin board, desk, or where you read or write letters.

Conservation Organizations:

Each of these organizations uses different strategies to help protect our environment. You'll have to investigate these organization(s) to find one or more whose philosophies and activities you can support wholeheartedly.

AuSable Institute of Environmental Studies (7526 Sunset Trail NE, Mancelona, MI 49659). Focus: environmental education from a biblical perspective.

Christian Nature Federation (P.O. Box 33,000, Fullerton, CA 92633; 714-447-9673). Focus: environmental awareness and Christian involvement.

Defenders of Wildlife (1244 Nineteenth Street NW, Washington, DC 20036; 202-659-9510). Focus: preserving native American plant and animal species.

Evangelical Lutheran Church in America (Commission for Church in Society, 8765 West Higgins Rd., Chicago, IL 60631-4190; 800-638-3522) Focus: church and environment, world hunger, and other social/economic issues.

Floresta, U.S.A., Inc. (1015 Chestnut Avenue, Suite F2, Carlsbad, CA 92008; 619-434-6311). Focus: reforestation as a ministry.

Global Greenhouse Network (1130 Seventeenth Street NW, Washington, DC 20036; 202-466-2823). Focus: global warming.

National Audubon Society (950 Third Avenue, New York, NY 10022; 212-832-3200). Focus: wildlife conservation.

National Geographic Society (Seventeenth and M Streets NW, Washington, DC 20036; 202-857-7000). Focus: environmental and geographic education for children and adults.

National Wildlife Federation (1412 Sixteenth Street NW, Washington, DC 20036; 202-637-3700). Focus: wildlife conservation.

Nature Conservancy (1815 Lynn Street, Arlington, VA 22209). Focus: land preservation for nature sanctuaries.

Rainforest Action Network (Suite A, 301 Broadway, San Francisco, CA 94133; 415-398-4404). Focus: tropical forests.

Sierra Club (730 Polk Street, San Francisco, CA 94109; 415-776-2211). Focus: preservation of wilderness areas.

Worldwatch Institute (1776 Massachusetts Avenue NW, Washington, DC 20036; 202-452-1999). Focus: global environmental issues.

World Wildlife Fund (1250 Twenty-fourth Street NW, Washington, DC 20037; 202-293-4800). Focus: protection of wildlife.